Dr. Tanya D. Whitehead

Disability Accommodations At School and Work:

Dr. Tanya D. Whitehead

Disability Accommodations At School and Work:

A Person-Centered Guidebook

VDM Verlag Dr. Müller

Impressum/Imprint (nur für Deutschland/ only for Germany)
Bibliografische Information der Deutschen Nationalbibliothek: Die Deutsche Nationalbibliothek
verzeichnet diese Publikation in der Deutschen Nationalbibliografie; detaillierte bibliografische
Daten sind im Internet über http://dnb.d-nb.de abrufbar.
Alle in diesem Buch genannten Marken und Produktnamen unterliegen warenzeichen-, marken-
oder patentrechtlichem Schutz bzw. sind Warenzeichen oder eingetragene Warenzeichen der
jeweiligen Inhaber. Die Wiedergabe von Marken, Produktnamen, Gebrauchsnamen,
Handelsnamen, Warenbezeichnungen u.s.w. in diesem Werk berechtigt auch ohne besondere
Kennzeichnung nicht zu der Annahme, dass solche Namen im Sinne der Warenzeichen- und
Markenschutzgesetzgebung als frei zu betrachten wären und daher von jedermann benutzt
werden dürften.

Coverbild: www.purestockx.com

Verlag: VDM Verlag Dr. Müller Aktiengesellschaft & Co. KG
Dudweiler Landstr. 99, 66123 Saarbrücken, Deutschland
Telefon +49 681 9100-698, Telefax +49 681 9100-988, Email: info@vdm-verlag.de

Herstellung in Deutschland:
Schaltungsdienst Lange o.H.G., Berlin
Books on Demand GmbH, Norderstedt
Reha GmbH, Saarbrücken
Amazon Distribution GmbH, Leipzig
ISBN: 978-3-639-24089-4

Imprint (only for USA, GB)
Bibliographic information published by the Deutsche Nationalbibliothek: The Deutsche
Nationalbibliothek lists this publication in the Deutsche Nationalbibliografie; detailed
bibliographic data are available in the Internet at http://dnb.d-nb.de .
Any brand names and product names mentioned in this book are subject to trademark, brand or
patent protection and are trademarks or registered trademarks of their respective holders. The use
of brand names, product names, common names, trade names, product descriptions etc. even
without a particular marking in this works is in no way to be construed to mean that such names
may be regarded as unrestricted in respect of trademark and brand protection legislation and
could thus be used by anyone.

Cover image: www.purestockx.com

Publisher:
VDM Verlag Dr. Müller Aktiengesellschaft & Co. KG
Dudweiler Landstr. 99, 66123 Saarbrücken, Germany
Phone +49 681 9100-698, Fax +49 681 9100-988, Email: info@vdm-publishing.com

Printed in the U.S.A.
Printed in the U.K. by (see last page)
ISBN: 978-3-639-24089-4

This book is dedicated to Bill Whitehead, who listens and supports with genuine interest; and in his honor- to all who listen.

Note:

The examples used in this material are not specific individuals but they are compilations of common situations, designed to help the reader understand how to conceptualize the challenges inherent in applying the "helping tools" presented.

TABLE OF CONTENTS

LIST OF TABLES

LIST OF FIGURES

CHAPTER 1: Person Centered Planning

An Introduction To The Concepts

The field of human services is not value free. The values a person holds impact the person's actions. What a person believes about human beings, interpersonal relationships and responsibility are very important when they enter a role in human services. If you are interested in the field of disability you probably already have a philosophical perspective on disability, beliefs about disability rights and opinions on your own responsibility as a member of society, even though you may not have written down these beliefs or expressed them to others.

In this book we will spend some time reviewing what experts in the field have written about personal values and the philosophy of human rights for accommodations in both education and work settings. There has been a long history of work in this field to describe the rights of persons with disabilities from a psychological or a philosophical perspective. As you read the book you will discover many new ideas that you may have not considered, yet.

As you read about the beliefs of others who work in the field you will begin to be able to put together your own original statement to clarify your personal belief system and this will help you find ways to express your philosophy to others.

Knowing about the thinking of leaders in the field and understanding the perspective of the people with disabilities who receive supports and services from the government and from agencies will help you clarify the role you, personally, want to take in working in the area of disability. You will be able to build a platform from which you can work based upon your new knowledge of the political and social realities of the field, and your own unique philosophical standpoint.

One of the most important things needed prior to a discussion of human rights is an understanding of the impact of words and language used to refer to disability and to persons with disability. This way of speaking about people is clearly based on our philosophical framework, which is an outgrowth of our beliefs about the value of people and the meaning of disability. The language we use to talk about disability must allow us to speak respectfully about accommodations for disability.

Language is powerful. The words used and the way that things are spoken about impacts the way others think about them.

For example, some people do not like the term "disability" because they believe it implies the person with that label is DIS- abled. That is to say, without ability. These people prefer to say that people are DIFFERENTLY- ENABLED and they believe that that to suggest otherwise is demeaning to people.

Other well meaning people believe that a disability is cultural rather than real. They believe that no one actually has a disability unless the people around them perceive them as "lesser" in some way. People who take this view prefer to use the word "challenge" for adults or the action based term "special needs" when referring to educational planning for a child. Still others prefer to avoid the terms "challenge" or "special need" because to their ears such terms imply patronization.

It is interesting, isn't it, that we have not come up with a term that satisfies everyone? We have not had that problem with the terms "handsome" or "beautiful". So, clearly, social stigma and the attempt to avoid stigmatizing labels must have something to do with the problems society has referring to disability in a way that does not offend anyone.

If there were a single term approved by everyone, I would use it. But since there is not, in this book we will utilize all three terms, depending upon the context. I will say "person with a disability" when I am writing about an issue that impacts people collectively as a segment of society or a political group. I will use the word "challenge" when I am talking about a barrier and how a student or an adult or person of working age along with their parents, employers, friends or other associates can identify and overcome a difficulty that is hindering their progress. The term "Children with Special Needs" is the term most often used in classrooms, so this term will be used largely in discussions about the classroom setting to help us clarify the classroom and educational accommodations that can render a classroom environment more suitable or teaching style more

11

effective or beneficial for children who have special needs in one or another specific area.

USE PEOPLE FIRST LANGUAGE

While there is not complete agreement on which specific terms should be utilized, almost everyone believes that the use of "people first" language is critical. In *people first language*, we put the person before the disability. For example, we would say, "a person with a diagnosis of Autism" rather than "an Autistic".

When you read over the two terms thoughtfully, it will be clear to you that the first term- "person with autism"- expresses respect for the person. It literally puts the person first. Putting the person first implies that there is a whole person with all the complexities, talents and issues that being a person implies- and then to that basic description a bit more information is added about the person: namely that the person also has a diagnosis of Autism.

Whereas the other way, without people first language, the sense of a whole person is lost and the only thing that comes across to the listener is the term Autism. Does it take a little longer to use people first language? Yes, it does, and certainly taking a few more milliseconds to avoid slighting someone is worth it.

In each section of the book, and anytime you refer to a person with a disability diagnosis we will use people first language.

PERSON CENTERED PLANNING

We will also take the value-based approach that people must be at the center of all of the planning done *with*, *by* and *for* them. The process by which it is made clear that people are at the center of their own plans is called *person-centered planning*, and it is a topic on which there has been a great deal written. Person centered planning first gained general acceptance in the very early 1990s and it has been of increasing importance ever since. Moving rapidly away from a completely <u>expert-driven system</u> by the year 2000, the field has reached the point in which it is the state of the art to use person-centered planning techniques during the annual planning meetings of adults using system services and supports.

Despite the acceptance of adults with disabilities as planners of their own lives, it is still a much less common practice in schools for children who have Individual Educational Plans or "IEPs". It is my hope that this mindset will gradually change. We might ask the question, "How are adults going to be able to gain the practice and experience in planning for themselves if they are marginalized in the process of planning throughout their childhoods?"

In addition to their own lack of experience in person centered planning, people using services are being "planned for", "evaluated", "assessed" and "modified" by staff who are not experienced either. Person-centered planning is actually more an art than it is a science, and people get better at it when they have lots of hands-on practice. So trying to use it in practice amongst large numbers of people by staff people who are marginally trained in the person-centered planning techniques and models is where we actually come up against a problem. The problems we face are partially from a lack of experience among the planners and partly from a hold-over of the old values in which persons with disabilities were not allowed to sit in the driver's seat during the planning processes in their own lives.

What is Person Centered Planning?

For those of you who aren't familiar with the person centered planning model, let's just start by answering this first question: What is person-centered planning? If you are experienced in the field of disability, you are very well aware that a person with a disability has things done to them or for them a great deal of the time. People have therapy given to them. They are driven places. Sometimes they receive intimate care in eating and dressing. People are taught. They are still being rewarded and punished in group settings.

While all of these things are being done *for* and *to* people, the interventions are often done in an "other centered" manner. "Other centered" means that the reason the activities are taking place is that

14

someone other than the person with the disability determined that the intervention was of value. Someone wanted a specific outcome for the person with a disability or from the person with the disability. So while the activities are certainly centered *around* the person, and services are delivered *to* the person, the activities were actually designed to meet the desires, the demands, the issues, the beliefs, the hopes, and the dreams of others. They are not person-centered.

Person-centered planning, then, is putting the person in the very center of every plan made for them so that the plan is not just for the person but it is about the person and it is by the person and it is designed to meet the beliefs, hopes, dreams and needs of the person who owns the plan.

Person-centered planning as an ideal arose when a group of people who had developmental disabilities and physical disabilities met. In talking about their lives as a group they found that they shared a number of common experiences related to the delivery of their supports and services.

One issue that resonates strongly with most people is their home. While people using services made it clear that they wanted to have a home of their own, they did not live in homes of their own. They lived in group settings which were selected by others. Most people lived, in fact, with roommates they did not choose to live with.

People knew that they didn't have the income needed to buy a house and live alone, but they wanted to live with a roommate of their own choosing. However, their wishes were not considered when their homes were set up. They were grouped together with other people whose need for services created a nice match in terms of available staffing by an agency.

A third issue that was cause for concern for many people who use disability services and supports is related to their work life. People sincerely wanted a real job in a community setting, and to have the freedoms taken for granted by the rest of this society. But again, people were required to work in institutionalized jobs, which had been negotiated for them collectively by their agency. People worked in jobs in which people were interchangeable rather than individually valued. They were assigned to jobs in settings designed to be convenient for agency staff to pick up and deliver clusters of people by van at set hours of the day. Rather than assuming real work most people held jobs which they realized were designed just to get them out of the way for some portion of every day.

As they talked among themselves people with disabilities realized that for a complex set of reasons related to the mistaken belief that people with disabilities need to be "fixed" in some way, their lives were forever constrained by requirements to reach goals set for them by others.

People with disabilities felt like perpetual children; always knowing that the next assessment was just around the corner and that it would be followed by the next behavior modification trial. In despair they realized that they would never be able to live an adult life of their own choosing in the community. Life did not have to be this way. People who face challenges and barriers to an independent life are not prevented from attaining autonomy by their challenges, they are prevented by societal circumstances. So their problems in attaining autonomous lives in the community are based on the value that others put on people with disabilities (that they are not capable), and the sense of expectations that others have for the performance of people with disabilities (which is generally very low).

So it follows that the *values* of the person-centered planning model are related to the issue of the moral right of a person with or without a disability to life, liberty and the pursuit of happiness.

Guiding Principle for Planning:

All Americans have the constitutional right to life, liberty and the pursuit of happiness!

Planning Basics

All of us plan for our own lives. From our early years people ask us what we want to be. People ask us what we want to do. People ask us our plans. We are the central person in our own lives. We may not always be wise. We may start one course of action and change our minds to take another course. Sometimes we fail. But there are few times anyone questions that we have the right to make our own plans. However, that sacred principle is not true for people who use disability services.

In traditional planning models for people with disabilities, the support person or the staff makes the plan that will rule the life of the person with a disability diagnosis. As H.R. Turnbull (1992) stated in the forward to "Crossing The River" (Schwartz, 1992) "we have not been human enough, we have been too mechanistic in our approaches to people with disabilities. We have relied too much and too exclusively on professionalism and advocacy. Yet we have not "cured" people with disabilities of their disability, or ourselves by our presence with them. What we must do, Schwartz says, is to be less the scientific rationalist and more the poet. We must be more the caring, open, vulnerable, risk-taking person" in order to serve as we ought. As service people, then we need to change our ways. Person-centered planning, is the first step we can take that puts the person with the disability in the driver's seat in their own life.

Once they really think about it, most people agree that person centered planning is a good idea at one level or another. But it can be a very difficult task to carry out. There are some important things to know before planning with others and in this chapter we are going to go over, step by step, how to create a person centered plan. We will also address its limitations. As we begin to think through the planning process we will review some actual plans and discuss how they were carried out, and

18

along the way we will explore the kinds of things that occur over time, that make person-centered planning so challenging.

Whether the planning process has been orderly or haphazard, every one of us has created (or we have stumbled upon) a preferred lifestyle ideal that we use as a guide in making plans for our own lives. That plan was not handed to us. We created the plan for ourselves with the help of people who are significant in our lives. No one came with a life plan already prepared for us, but every one of us has figured out goals for ourselves as we went along and we have struggled and sometimes soared as we attempted to reach them. With the input of parents, teachers, and friends we set goals, try to reach them, sometimes fail, sometimes revise our plan, and always persevere in planning for ourselves.

There is a lot about person centered planning that you already know, because you are already building a person centered plan for your own life. Person-centered planning may simply be an unfamiliar label for a very familiar activity. Certainly the tasks of person centered planning are well known to every adult in the world. In our personal planning processes we have thought through what we want. We have asked ourselves what work we want to do or whether or not we want to earn a college degree. It may be that one person-centered plan for your life is to finish your education. Maybe you've planned a marriage or a family. Maybe you've planned to start a new business or take a trip to Europe. You are looking ahead. Some of your plans may take years to accomplish.

19

People, with and without disabilities, have multiple levels of plans with outcomes they expect to reach over time. Plans grow, change and develop over time. Sometimes we start with one course of action and decide against completing it as we discover it is not as fulfilling as we had expected it to be. That is all part of the learning process through which we pass as we move through the years.

While the person is at the center of the plan, no matter what the goal might be, none of us can reach our goals alone. We are all interdependent. And while planning is a familiar process for everyone, helping someone else plan is a more formal process than most of us are used to. It is more formal because people with disabilities who use system services and supports have a team of staff responsible for specific areas of the person's life, and there is usually a guardian, as well. People often find that the planning process is encumbered both by the regularities of a service system and by the personalities and preferences of a person's staff and their family. Issues related to transportation, how busy everyone's schedules are, and other logistics can add layers of challenge to the planning process. It is little wonder that a person can easily become lost amidst the sea of paperwork and layers of bureaucracy designed to take care of them.

The goal of the planning process for people with disabilities is simple: just put the person at the center of the planning process! But carrying out the planning process is not simple. If it were easy it would have been done, already.

Everyone on the planning team has a role to play. The person is where the energy needs to come from for that plan. People must learn to dream big for their own lives, and to work toward goals that are personally meaningful to them. Even before a formal planning starts, the person must take the lead by wanting to develop a personal plan and by designing their own "Executive Board", so to speak, their Planning Team. The person has the right to determine with which people they want share the process of planning.

Whether the Planning Team is composed of relatives, friends, staff or others, the person should have the right and does have the right, to choose with whom they do their planning. When people plan they are going to choose team members they trust; people in whom they have confidence; and maybe most importantly of all, they are going to choose people that they trust will listen to them and accept their ideas. They will choose a planning team that they believe will help them reach their goals because the members of the team have demonstrated over time that they will support the person on every level.

A planning team needs to have at least three people on it, and some have many more. Having more than nine members of the team may make it hard for everyone to feel truly needed and committed to the follow through.

As shown in Table 1, if there are more than nine people that you want to have on your Planning Team you might consider setting service terms for your team, and rotate your friends and relatives on- and- off of active status on the team. That works well for the team members who are very busy with their own lives. It lets them concentrate on working with you for some months (usually 18 – 24 months) and then they can take a breather.

Choosing who is on the team is vital. You don't want to have people in the planning group that aren't going to be able to put some elbow grease into this plan and help make it become a reality. You have to have people in the planning process that will commit to helping carry out the plans that the person has come up with, but you don't want to let people get burned out.

So planning to rotate people on-and-off of active planning status on your team is a good idea.

Table 1: Members of the Planning Team

MEMBERS OF THE PLANNING TEAM are about nine in number. *They are*:
• Chosen by the person whose plan it is • Chosen because they have proven that they will listen

- Chosen because they care deeply about the person and support them emotionally
- Chosen because they will dedicate themselves to helping carry out the plan, once it is made

And afterward, they listen again- to see when it is time to rethink the plan.

The planning team can actually use the planning process to help develop the person's priorities. This can be difficult to do because a person may want to do a number of different things, and they may not have had practice in setting priorities for their goals. For example: a person may want to go to school, get married, start a family, move to Seattle and open a business – all good and interesting things to do. But no one could do all of those things tomorrow. Each goal will take a different length of time in the maturation process so that each part of the plan can become a reality. While each of those plans may overlap to some extent, most of them take so much time and energy that no one could do them all simultaneously.

So the planning process then may start with a brainstorm of where this person wants their life to go first. In the first stages of planning everyone should just listen to the person dream aloud, and take notes. Once the goals are written down, the team can help to prioritize the goals. When the goals set out on paper, the person is in the driver's seat; they can plan which of the goals to work on first, which second and so on. The person who is planning is now in control and the other planners take their cues from the person as to what steps are needed to reach each goal, and when. Like everyone else, a person with a disability is interdependent, not independent. We all need others to help us make our goals a reality. No one can go it alone.

Guiding Principle for Planning:

Person-centered planning needs to be specifically built upon the unique wishes, preferences, desires, hopes, dreams, and abilities of the person whose plan it is.

Now that everyone clearly understands the process of creating a person centered plan, it is time to discuss some of the difficulties that might arise during the planning process.

The Planning Process: the agony and the ecstasy

The first issue in planning is to determine whether or not the person whose plan it is has a guardian.

Most children and many adults have parents or guardians who will be part of the planning process. Those children whose parents are not active in their lives have educational advocates or foster parents. Some adults have had their civil rights withdrawn by the court after they were adjudicated "incompetent". Some adults know their guardian and others who have a guardian don't know who it is.

For example there are 4,000 people living in my county who are wards of the state. Most of these 4,000 people have been assigned to one single guardian, the public administrator, who is completely responsible for all decisions about their medical care, education, living circumstances and work settings. The guardian must supply a signature of approval for every detail in the lives of these 4,000 souls in areas ranging from their personal spending allowance to major decisions about their medical care.

Most people have a guardian who has far fewer wards. The guardian decides what level of intervention is a medical necessity and when treatment will not be given, as well as signing off on accommodation, employment and social plans.

As you can easily see the guardian fills an enormously powerful position in a person's life, and yet the guardian and the ward in many cases are not even acquainted. However, even if the guardian is not known to the person, the guardian's written approval is required on every official action taken by the person, so the involvement of the guardian must be sought from the first stages of planning.

As shown in Table 2, providing the right documents to the guardian (and at the right times) will help greatly in leading to a successful planning outcome.

25

Table 2: How To Involve A Guardian In A Successful Planning Process

Write a letter to the guardian and ask the guardian to be a member of the planning team.
Inform the guardian about the planning team. Include a list of team members and their business and home contact numbers as well as their relationship to the person who is planning.
Give the guardian a list of all meeting times for the year to come, for their file.
Add the guardian to the Document Mailing List. You don't have to send the guardian a copy of every little email between people, but be sure to send the original invitation, the minutes of the meeting and the agenda to the guardian after every planning session.
Make sure you don't try to rush the guardian. If it looks like the person is preparing a major change of residence or job, or wants to marry, inform the guardian of their interests well in advance of any meetings on the subject.
Send copies of all of the paperwork related to the guardian well before they are needed, and provide a rich documentation that supports the wisdom of the proposed change.

So not only do parents and guardians have to be involved in planning, additionally, there must be someone on the planning team who has the time and the energy and can make a commitment to follow through with carrying out the plans as made. Some guardians will be very active. Others will designate someone else to act in their stead. Having active members on the team who will dedicate themselves to follow through is critical for the success of the plan, because the only thing worse than not planning with someone at all is planning with them but failing to see the plan through so that the person's dreams can become a reality.

In A Nutshell

Person Centered Planning is an attitude based on our high regard for human rights for every person. It could be a call for a change in attitude among some of the people working with someone who has a disability.

Experts have gotten used to doing things for people with special needs. But person-centered planning is not built around the guidance of experts, it puts the person in the driver's seat. In this type of planning the expert is the person whose plan it is.

In carrying out person centered planning we are not looking for an expert or specialist to tell us that someone needs to be rewarded or punished for eating too much or for not eating enough. We don't want an expert or specialist to tell us someone needs to learn to follow directions, or to shower or go to bed when they are told to. This is not the place for anyone to emphasize all of the things a person "can't do". What we need instead is an emphasis on listening to the person who owns the plan, and then creating a planning and implementation team to help the person establish the connections in the community that will support them as they move into their plan.

Of course a person will rely a great deal upon their own abilities, but personal relationships and community networks play a role in everyone's life. Through the process of planning and building a community-based, purpose-driven life the team will learn by trial and error to creatively solve problems and surmount barriers to progress.

Person centered planning does not mean the person must "go it alone"! The person whose plan it is serves as the leader but they are not "independent", if independent means they are alone. We are all interdependent. Not one of us can get through our life without the support or help of others.

Guiding Principle for Planning:

American public policy and attitude towards disability shows signs of change.

In fact, legislation now protects the rights of people with disabilities to live meaningful, interdependent lives in the community, lives of their own choosing.

Strengths Model

As you can easily see, those who carry out person-centered planning believe that people should be talked about, and thought about, and interacted with based on their strengths and their interests, their gifts and their contributions. In fact, the person leads this type of discussion!

No matter what barriers a person may face in their life, each one also has strengths, interests, gifts and talents. Planning starts with the person's strengths, that is: what the person likes to do and wants to do. If the goals are based upon what their abilities are and, most importantly, what their interests are people will be motivated to work very hard to achieve them.

The planning is person-centered only when the planners listen to the desires of the person and the plan is based upon their interests, talents, and strengths. When the planners are willing to take action to help the person bring about a desired change in their life you know you are looking at a person-centered plan.

It's critical to focus on this last point for just a moment. Planning alone does not change people's lives. After the plan, there must be action. You can have the best plan in the world but the person's life will remain the same until follow through takes place and things get done. So the focus of the planning process has to be on who should take action, and when and how the action steps that will make the plan a reality will take place.

Planning is just the beginning. It must be followed by action directed to carry out the initial phase of the plan. And planning is not a one-time event. After the initial steps of action have taken place another meeting is held to review and evaluate the action and its outcomes. Based upon progress to date, plans are revised, enhanced or even changed to lead to a robust outcome. Depending upon the type of planning underway, planning teams may meet monthly with weekly or even daily emails and calls.

At the very least, planning teams meet annually to assure that prior progress is maintained and that future events and potential needs are discussed. As the planning team matures, it learns to gradually adjust itself to the rhythm of the process of planning, plans are adjusted as they unfold, and gradually a more effective team is able to help the person build a rich and satisfying life.

A Note About Listening

During planning the team needs to listen from the "strengths model" explained above. As we listen to someone share their hopes and dreams for their life, we learn to view the person being planned with as a powerful person, a "can-do" person, an outspoken person with great talents and strengths. No matter what barriers we observe, we refuse to assume that something desired can not be achieved. We are listening with an open mind.

There are many ways to listen, but not all of them are effective. In order to discover our own listening skills we have to observe ourselves closely. There are listening errors that actively prevent us from hearing what the other person wants to communicate. Perhaps you have also heard an exchange like the one below:

Staff: "What do you want to eat for dinner? We've got Macaroni and Cheese here, already cooked."

Person who lives in the group home says, "Yew! That's leftovers!"

Staff: "OK, so it's Mac and Cheese tonight! After dinner you can watch TV until 8:00 PM."

While the exchange may serve to get the meal out of the way, it is not an example of good listening. Why did the staff ask the person what they want to eat if she was not going to listen to what they say and then serve the person what they wanted? Could it be that her job specifies that she must ask, but that she did not want to go to the trouble of cooking a fresh meal and the job does not specify that she must? Is it possible that she changed the topic to television immediately after telling the person she works for that their meal would be left over macaroni and cheese to remind them that she could revoke their television privilege if they made a fuss?

A great deal is communicated without words, simply by the way we listen and the response we make to the communication of others.

The steps of listening are clear: a question is asked. Then there is silence while you stop talking so you can hear what the other person's response is. People who want to serve on planning teams must observe their own listening habits as part of the preliminary training process so that they can learn about their habits and find ways to improve them, if needed.

Communication can be difficult. A childhood friend, exactly my age, lived two houses down the street. Johnny and I played together all summer and every day after school. He was one of my best friends, even though he was a boy and I was a girl. I saw Johnny as a loving friend. He was loyal, funny, good natured, generous, helpful, and kind. Any part of the game that depended upon Johnny was always faithfully carried out.

I was surprised to find that other people thought Johnny had a communication disability that was too difficult to surmount. People would act as though they could not understand him at all. Instead of speaking to Johnny, they would ask me, instead. "Does Johnny want a popsicle?" Johnny would get frustrated when people didn't understand him. If he was upset he found it harder to speak clearly, or if he was using a new word or if I hadn't seen him for several days sometimes even I would forget the systematic way Johnny changed the sounds of words. Then I would have to say, "What?" At those times he would get mad at me, because he counted on me to understand everything he said.

I remember saying to him when we were about eight, "Johnny, I'm listening as hard as I can. You are talking as hard as you can. Let's just keep trying until we get it right." When I said that, he smiled at me, his dark brown eyes twinkling with friendly lights, and we shook hands on the promise.

It takes commitment to stand quietly and listen. It disrupts momentum as it slows things down a notch. But if you don't learn to listen "as hard

32

as you can", you will certainly miss some very worthwhile communications. With some practice on their side, and some practice on yours, communication problems can be readily surmounted.

Besides simple articulation differences, other things may interfere and keep someone from communicating with you as well. One frequently encountered issue is that many people with disabilities have a long history of finding that nobody is listening to them, so they've either given up trying to say what they mean. Sometimes when people with disabilities have shared their thoughts they have found that their own preferences are used against them (as rewards or punishments) so they have wisely decided to keep their feelings and ideas secret.

An issue that gets in the way of communication is the long history of punishment that has been inflicted upon people who live institutionalized lives.

Some people have an understanding of the role they have innocently played in their own punishment. When they have shared this insight with me they feel a mixture of shame, rage and fear. It makes them distrust those "in charge" and inhibits communication. An example of this occurs in some group homes and residential settings as well as in places of employment and education. A person may innocently tell people, "I like to watch this movie or this TV show; or I like to eat that food; or I like to listen to this radio station. It is very, very unfortunate that in a token economy setting the item that they have confided that they like is taken

33

away from them, so that it can be used as a reward for doing what someone else wants them to do.

The opportunity to watch a TV show one likes, or listen to the radio should be a human right. However, in a token economy environment people are no longer entitled to listen to a radio station they like. They have to earn the privilege. They are no longer entitled to eat something that they like and they are no longer entitled to watch a TV show that they like. Such things become something they have to earn based on "good" behavior; that is, earned "points" for "being good" and doing what one is told to do. I have known people who taught themselves to stop communicating voluntarily at all, because *in their reality* communication, which is a fundamental human need, simply isn't safe.

As you can see there are a number of different reasons why people might have trouble talking and communicating. Some of these reasons are part of the persons' unique challenge, and others are learned or situational. However, despite the difficulties imposed by physical or emotional barriers to communication most people want to communicate. It is a natural human need common to us all. Many people who have lived institutional lives have had that need suppressed for years for one reason or another. The burden should not be on them to "try harder to say it the right way". The burden is on the team to listen more skillfully and to value and respect the information that is being communicated to us by verbal and nonverbal means.

What makes a good planning team member?

It is flattering to be invited to join a Person Centered Planning Team by someone who trusts us to share their life planning. Sometimes people are appointed to the team by their boss. When it is part of a person's job to serve on a planning team, is somewhat less flattering than an invitation. However, since the person deserves to have only committed and caring team members the invitee should decline unless they can serve with the same commitment that a family member or friend would have.

It's important for potential team members to decide ahead of time how involved they will be able to become. If the team members don't think ahead on their time commitment parameters, the person could be set up to believe that they are going to be able to have someone's time available to them, when they really aren't. From the very beginning the communication has to be clear: people must communicate what the expectations of the person is for his or her team, and what level of time and energy each team member will have available for working on the plan. It's very important that from the beginning the limitations of each person's involvement are clear to everybody.

During the meetings the team members have to work hard at communicating roles and responsibilities for each of the members. People need to know what is expected of them and everybody must be in agreement on what actions need to be taken by each team member within a given timeframe. Someone on the team has to take responsibility for group communications by email, mail or phone. Everyone has to know what the next steps are at the end of the planning process.

Since the Person Centered Planning will have to unfold over time, and since it takes repeated, heartfelt, earnest, long-term planning to make things really change in someone's life, a service term of 12 to 18 months should be established for most team members. Team members can transition over a period of many months so that there are always both old and new team members on the board.

Person Centered Planning Tools

Person Centered Planning was developed to help people with developmental disabilities plan for their own lives in response to a situation in which under existing social conditions agencies have developed programs for people, rather than helping people develop plans for lives of their own.

A basic assumption underlying the Person Centered Planning process is that the authority about the person rests within that person, not within someone else (Bozarth, 1991)[1]. Person Centered Planning is a "bottom-up" tool which assists people in learning to design their own lives, with input from others whom they trust. It provides a process of discussion and self-evaluation during which a person discovers how they want to live (Smull, Sanderson, & Harrison, 1996)[2] and during which the person's friends help them to explore what needs to be done in order to reach their goals.

> **Guiding Principle for Planning:**
> Person Centered Planning is not a product. It is an on-going process during which learning and growth occur as people gradually get the opportunities they need.
> Michael Smull[1]

Traditional planning entrusts the planning for people with developmental disabilities to the hands of "experts". The problem with this type of life planning is that the outcomes important to experts are not individual in nature, but are assessments for quality on standardized outcomes.

Self Advocates and the people who support them want to move away from the idea that the person is the problem and needs to be fixed. If the person is seen as "broken" in some way, it would make sense for experts to make the decisions to support the person according to what is believed to be best for them.

However, under this model of planning, if the plan is miserable for someone it would be only natural for them to fight against the plan. If a person receiving services starts fighting the system, behavior modification techniques and medications are used to control them. The more miserable they are with the plan, the more they try to circumvent

---

[1] M. Smull. (1995). After The Plan. AAMA News and Notes. Jan. Vol. 8. No. 1

the plan, and the greater their punishment. According to Towson (1996)[2] even in "good" programs standardized outcomes will fail at the personal level since preferred outcomes are always unique to each individual and when outcomes do fail, the person is identified as the problem.

As Mount has stated (1994)[3] person centered planning can not occur in a vacuum. It requires people and systems to value and respect the right of all people to develop their strengths and to live satisfying lives of their own choosing in the community.

The tools of person centered planning do not provide a quick fix to the problems facing people with developmental disabilities as they learn to design a lifestyle that makes sense to them. It is a complex task.

It can be a slow and laborious process for people to create viable life plans for themselves. Since many people have known only institutional lives, they lack the life experience to make informed choices or understand the intensity of work that follow through will require.

The great news is that over the past twenty years or so, with the emergence of self advocacy in the developmental disability community people have been increasingly seeking self determination and the right to choose where they live and work, and to select their own staff. Person

---

[2] M. Towson (1996) Update on Quality. The Accreditation Council. Vol 3, No.2

[3] M. Mount. (1994) Benefits and Limitations of Personal Futures Planning. Ch. 6. Pages 97-108.

Centered Planning is not an attempt to reverse the old pattern in which the system had power over the individuals that they served, but a new model in which all interested parties develop common goals, common values and work together for both short and long-term goals.

The benefit of person centered planning is that within this positive view of people, they are able to discover their strengths, talents, and interests and learn to work toward maximizing their contribution to society.

The Person Centered Plan is never finished.

There are a number of unique planning tools designed to help groups focus their efforts through a clear and streamlined process. There are differences between the planning tools, because each one may be most helpful in one or another specific area. However, all of the planning tools and strategies have one thing in common: the effectiveness of the person centered plan depends upon there being a support group of concerned and committed people who will help the individual implement their goals, learn to identify and address problems as they arise, and build community, over time.

Table 3: Planning Tools

NAME OF TOOL		USE OF TOOL
Personal Futures Planning	Mount	Teams of people who care about the individual are invited to

		share in the planning process lead by the individual. This group offers emotional and practical support to the person as they carry out their plans to reach their own life goals.
Lifestyle Planning	O'Brien	A planning process which focuses on essential outcomes of the individual's choice, with community presence and participation. A belief in the individual's competence and a respect for their strengths drive this model.
McGill Action Planning System (MAPS)	Vandercook	This system is a mechanism to arrange for students' inclusion in regular education classrooms. The planning circle consists of a team of peers, family, regular education and special education teachers who work together to answer seven questions with will focus on goal setting and the development of strategies that will provide the supports a child needs to learn in the regular

		education classroom.
Lifestyle Plan	Powell	This is an adaptation of O'Brien's Lifestyle Planning to include career goals. This six step planning process involves brainstorming and action planning to offer guidance to the individual in the early stages of employment. It was further adapted by Steer, et al (1993) to help young people between the ages of 14 – 20 in planning the initial transition to work.

Hard Learned Lessons in Planning

Guiding Principles for Planning:

1. There are some limits to planning with others.

2. Sometimes the plan doesn't work the way people hoped it would.

3. You can't make somebody's wishes come true.

4. As much as you wish you had a magic wand and could make only good things happen, you just can't.

Hard Learned Lesson 1: A Case In Which A Magic Wand Might Have Been Useful

At the time my friend Mr. Smith was born there was no public education for children with special needs. There were a number of challenges in his life. First, his parents were not part of his life, but fortunately he lived with elderly grandparents who sincerely wanted the best for him. Additionally, he was living in an urban core community, with an income level below the poverty line.

A social worker came to help, when the family came to the attention of the city government during a house fire. The social worker told them about a "state school" for children with disabilities, and his grandmother signed the papers thinking that she was providing him with an education. In fact, it was a state institution to which he was sent, and he was never given an education of any kind. He was put to work feeding stock and cleaning. When I met him Mr. Smith had lived in the institution from the age of nine years to the age of forty. After he was taken from his home at the age of nine, he only saw his Grandmother one more time because she did not have a car and could not drive the 90 miles from her home to the institution.

When the system released large numbers of people in the late 1970s Mr. Smith caught the wave and was sent to a nursing home in the city in which he had lived with his grandparents, now deceased. He had been upgraded to live in a group home by the time I met him, but he wanted an

42

apartment of his own. His memories of life with his grandparents lead him to dream of a home of his own, complete with a wife. He wanted to be married and have a happy family life.

When Mr. Smith was able to put together a person centered plan, he brought that goal to the table for his team to hear. In planning there are many things you can do. You can, in fact, help the planner get a home of his own, but the marriage is beyond the realm of our ability. There are some wishes you just can't make come true. You can help move people in the direction where the goal might become a reality. You can help connect people with singles groups and introduce people to each other and take all kinds of other assistance, but you just can't make their wishes for marriage come true. In the case of Mr. Smith, he met a woman he wanted to marry. She wanted to marry him to. Although her parents were in agreement, Mr. Smith's guardian would not allow the marriage to take place.

Hard Learned Lesson 2: People can be disappointed, even when they get what they want.

You know from events in your own life that sometimes, even when you get what you want, it is disappointing after all. Sometimes people will come up with a plan but it doesn't work as they hoped it would. There are time that we can't get what we really want, even when the plan seems to be working out fine.

For example: I had a friend who has a physical and cognitive disability. When he was in his late 60s he wanted to go to Israel, which he called The Holy Land. It was all he talked about for a long time. Finally his sister and members of her church raised the funds and my friend was able to go to the Holy Land with the church group, just as he wished. One of the main things he wanted to do while he was there was to be baptized in the River Jordan. As fortune would have it, my friend was able to be baptized in the River Jordan exactly as he hoped, as well.

What no one knew at the time was that my friend believed with all his heart that when he came up out of the River Jordan after being baptized, his body would be healed of Cerebral Palsy. He believed that the baptism would heal him and that his arms and legs would match on both sides and that he would have full vigor and strength on the right side as well as on the left.

When this did not happen for him, he was crushed. In the end, even though he got what he said he wanted, it didn't make his wishes come true. He did not share the whole dream with us (and that is OK, of course) but we were not aware that a huge disappointment awaited him because we did not know the real dream that lay under the part of the dream he shared with us.

Hard Learned Lesson 3: Sometimes people want things that are mutually exclusive.

You already know about this one. We say, "You can't have your cake and eat it too." Sometimes we all want two things but we can't have them both. It really is impossible, at times, to get exactly what we want because we want two things that simply can not co-exist. That fact has to be faced. It's just part of the learning and growing process. An example of this is planning with a person who wants to lose weight. However, they are unwilling to eat fewer calories, fewer grams of fat, and fewer desserts. If we make a plan to achieve a goal, but are not willing to take the steps necessary to obtain it, we are heading for disappointment. It is OK to make the goal and try, but we have to accept that there is work that has to be done each and every day to reach any meaningful goal. In a case like this one- it's back to the drawing board!

Hard Learned Lesson 4: You can't always get other people to do what you want them to do, even if it is the right thing and you know they should do it.

It can be very frustrating, but sometimes people don't do what you think they should do. They don't even do what they know they should do. That's just how life is. Even if they know they should, people don't always do what they know they should do.

45

You sometimes can not get some family members or staff people to change the way they interact with people in their homes unless they have a change of heart. Sometimes you can not get the biology teacher to use accommodations for a person with disabilities unless the teacher somehow has a change of heart. You can't make people do things even if they should do them, and that fact has to be accepted as one of the limitations in planning with other people that will come up from time to time.

When a really good plan is in place, sometimes the team will come up against a person in the community who is in the position to help, but they withhold the help the team needs. So the mindset of the team has to be "we are going to try this but it may not necessarily work out the first time. We may have to revise our plan and try again."

Sometimes important people like parents, guardians and staff are worried about how to accept change and their fear makes the act in ways that prevents the plan from working. Sometimes it is related to the number of people that a staff member has on his or her case load. The staff wants to "be fair to everyone" they say. They feel that they can't possibly do what is asked for this one person and then not do as much for everyone else. Others may want to keep out of the way for reasons of their own. Sometimes people are just lazy. They may say, "Well, I don't know enough about this to get involved in it."

People have good reasons for the way they act. Parents and guardians may think that they are not doing their chief job, which is protecting the person, if they let him or her take risks. Other times they may feel hurt, or somewhat pushed aside and forgotten if the person seems to be moving on and becoming less dependent. It can all be quite challenging, at times. Being a member of a Person Centered Planning Team has all the same interpersonal conflicts of any other group process.

Sometimes even good ideas don't work out.

But just because it didn't work doesn't mean it was a bad idea. It might have been a great idea but sometimes even good ideas don't work out for any one of a number of reasons. When that happens the team has to get back down to the drawing board. Sometimes people do want impossible things but sometimes what people want that seems impossible really isn't. You have to try it to find out.

Conflicts on the Team

There are going to be conflicts among team members from time to time. Each member comes to the table from a perspective that differs from the others in many ways. For example, people have many different values, they are accustomed to different practices, and they have learned to operate under different types of policy. The person who owns the plan may find they are in conflict with each of the team members at one time or another. From our experience in planning we have learned that some of the perspectives of various member types can be predicted. If you can predict, you can sometimes take steps to help people work better together so the planning process will go more smoothly.

One predictable problem relates to the concerns about safety held by many family members. Family members and guardians often want to protect the person even if their idea of protection means that the person is never allowed to set their own meaningful goals or work towards accomplishing independence.

Another group that sometimes finds it hard to help are those who are paid to be there. Service providers may be wedded to their common practices, and they want to uphold the policies and preferences of their agency or their own preferences rather than to put the person first. They are concerned about the time tasks might take, they are concerned about additional expense. They don't like to deal with people changing their minds because that creates more work. Agency staff may be concerned about doing what would seem to be fair when the services requested by one consumer are compared to services offered to other consumers. Agencies often want to avoid agreeing to something that will turn out to change a schedule or make more work for staff, or might cause other consumers to ask for changes in their own services.

In general when there is conflict it is often because the agency is most comfortable doing things the way they have always been done, or because family members often want something different for the person than what the person wants for his or herself.   Most of the time the plans a team draws up are quite modest and doable. But they always are based upon someone in the life of the person making a change, and that can be an unwelcome request.

In once such example a gentleman who was aged about 50, and who had lived in an institution from his childhood until the first wave of institutional release in the late 1970s. When he was released from the institution and placed in the community it was into a group home as a middle-aged adult.To his great surprise and delight, he met a woman in her 40s, with a similar disability, who was living in a nearby group home. These two people fell in love. The two wanted to marry and have an apartment of their own. The woman's family was in agreement but the man's family said that he could not marry. Although he was 50 years old, and had been in an institution for most of his life, a niece he hardly knew was his guardian. A guardian is legally in the position to allow or disallow all life decisions. This created a conflict in planning for this gentleman's team.

From time to time, there are going to be conflicts with families, conflicts with service providers, a doctor or a dentist that says, "I'm sorry. I understand what you want, but it is not allowed by our rules." Such conflicts come up around homes and lifestyles; travel; medication and medical treatment; education and employment. There are times when someone will reference a common practices policy to show the group why it is OK that they won't work with the person's person centered plan.

It is up to the team to determine how to deal with these conflicts. When these problems come up, each team needs to address each circumstance individually. The goal is to figure out how work things out with "*the powers that be*" in people's lives so that they can continue to move slowly and steadily toward lives that are meaningful and rich.

Guiding Principle for Planning:

The best goal in a conflict situation, is to seek ways to transform the conflict so that all parties may be uplifted and brought closer to a sense of their common interest.

Mahatma Gandhi

There isn't any way to avoid conflict entirely, but there are usually creative ways to manage conflict. Just a little bit of tolerance all around and an attempt to truly understand the other person's perspective may be very, very helpful in that regard because person-centered planning is a forum in which there are discussions about social roles, power and investments.

There is a component power in every relationship. Where the larger share of the power is balanced becomes very apparent when the family and the person, the employer and the professional helper, and/ or the school meet together. When there is a difference of opinion that cannot be remediated through discussion; when one side or the other digs in its heels; the polarization always hurts the person who owns the plan. These things take time to work out so that even when prevented from setting the goal they really have, the person is able to achieve something similar.

In the case of the gentleman who wanted to marry his girlfriend, it would have worked out for everyone if they had been able to hold a religious marriage ceremony and set up a home together, even if the family of the gentleman was afraid of a legally binding marriage. However, the guardian and his family extended their concern even so far as to prohibit cohabitation, so the gentleman was forced to carry on a relationship with his lover that he felt did not give her the respect she deserved.

What is Choice?

You hear a lot about "choice" when you are reading about person-centered planning. Sometimes really complicated ideas are given simple, casual words that add to the confusion. Choice is just such a word.

Some people think "choice" means the right to select from between two options. Others believe it means the right to set one's own ideas into motion. The word "choice" in the context of person centered planning and is a word that acts as a spotlight; showing clearly the intentions of the system in its management of a system of supports and services.

When people put themselves in danger, it's not a choice. It's a risk.

When people want to make decisions about where to live, where to work, what to eat and how to dress, it's a choice.

In one group home a particular person in my group was constantly being arrested for shoplifting at the nearby Wal-Mart. She had been arrested so many times that local law enforcement were talking about putting the person in jail. After stopping the woman who was shoplifting at the door many, many times and speaking to the staff repeatedly, the store and local police did not know what else to do, although they felt badly about it.

From the perspective of the staff, they felt that they were giving their "consumer" (or client) the "choice" that regulations require. They allowed the woman to go by herself to Wal-Mart every day because she wanted to do so, even after repeated episodes of shoplifting had occurred. When the police called home, the staff said, "Well, it's her choice. If she wants to be arrested and put in jail, that's her choice."

However, the woman who was shoplifting had little understanding of what being arrested would be like. She did not have a clear understanding that a trial, a legal conviction and having to serve time in jail meant that she would be locked in a cell. She was not able to imagine the impact on her future of a criminal record. If a vulnerable person is endangering himself or herself by their actions, they have a right to be protected from the subsequent injury, of which they are unaware, that they are inflicting upon themselves.

What is choice and how can we know at what point it might become risk? Building a life that is personally meaningful is not a choice. It's a right that is guaranteed by our government and it can be done in a way that limits exposure to risk.

Choice in person centered planning stands upon the adherence to a set of value based processes. The central value is the right of the person to autonomy (making up one's own mind and carrying out one's own plans).

Choice is considered to be "informed" when it meets the following criterion. Choice is:

1. A decision based on personal preference after learning what the options are (informed)

2. An informed decision based on knowledge of potential outcomes from the choice

3. Knowledge of how to evaluate goal directed activities success periodically

When working with people who are vulnerable it is critical that the people supporting others and the people around them and contributing to their success are aware of the nature of the vulnerability and are willing to take a stand on behalf of the person's rights; both their right to choice and their right for protection.

Choice must be meaningful. Sometimes a narrow range of options are presented as choices that are so meaningless that they don't count as a choice. True choice is a stated preference that arises from the person.. Choice is not a selection from among a narrow range of proffered options.

Meaningful Choice: Where You Live

A primary example of an important meaningful choice is deciding where to live, who one's own roommate is, and how to manage household tasks. Many people who receive system supports and services are placed in apartments and shared rooms with strangers. Agency staff make decisions based upon what is good for the business, rather than the preferences of the people.

In this disempowering process, people are informed of the change in their home life either by letters that they cannot read, or by word of mouth.

If you put yourself in their place for a moment, you can imagine the devastation of coming home one day to find out that you are going to be moved to another apartment for the convenience of the business that provides your services. People need to feel comfortable in their homes, and they need to feel secure that things won't change unless they want them to.

If you came home on the agency van from your job in a sheltered workshop, and someone told you that you were being moved to a new home, you would wait anxiously to meet your new roommate.

A roommate is a person with whom you would be expected to spend all of your leisure time. This yet unknown person is someone who will be given access to all of your belongings and someone with whom you will lay asleep in bed, at your most vulnerable. From your extensive experience in living with strangers you know that there will be issues that arise. Perhaps your roommate will want the electric light turned on far into the night, past the time when you want to sleep. Perhaps you will want to listen to a radio or CD but your roommate wants to sleep. You hope you do not get assigned someone who likes to eat in bed because that makes the room smell of stale food.

But you know it is all out of your hands. You will have no say in the matter. If you complain, you will get "written up" or punished.

Meaningful Choice: Who Works For You

Who is it that is entitled to make these decisions that impact people at such deep levels of their lives? It is agency staff.

Staff members are very important figures in the lives of people who need supports and services. Some people only need a little support for tasks like balancing their checkbooks, making arrangements for medical care, and transportation. Others, though, need help in personal areas such as dressing, eating, and using the bathroom. The staff members serving this group are an intimate part of their experience in life and they have the right to choose who those staff people are. In fact, the staff works for the person with a disability. It is the person who is funded through the government, and the person's money pays the staff.

In common practice, though, staff members believe that they work for an agency rather than for the person who uses their services. While the agency exists solely on the dollars Congress appropriated to people with disabilities, meaning that the agency works for the people, over time the agency has usurped the position of power. Once the agency convinced the government that it should send the person's check right to the agency, the person has become, in effect, a ward of the agency rather than the client of the agency whom the agency exists to serve.

Again, instead of the person receiving the government check and then paying their staff each month, the government sends the check directly to the agency. Since people do not pay their agency staff by check each month, the agency has forgotten that it works for the person.

Since the agency receives the funds directly from the government, in fact, the agency now takes what it wants from the person's check and then releases funds back to the person according to how much the agency believes the person has proven they can manage. So the agency staff give an allowance of their own money to the person and keeping the rest "for their own good".

The agency now has established how things will be done. Instead of the more direct and clear method of the person with a disability selecting personal care and support staff who will meet their own personal standards of preference, the agency head selects staff and assigns them to people based upon a process that works best for the agency. The result is that many people are living institutional-like lives, even in community settings.

Meaningful Choice: Where You Work

Most people with developmental disabilities have lived their lives under a cloud of discrediting prophecies and assessment outcomes that seem to prove they will never amount to much.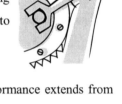

The low expectations others hold for their performance extends from school into their working lives without question, in most cases. Most people with developmental disabilities are either unemployed or work in sheltered workshops or group jobs (such as maid service at a hotel).

However, people who are *differently enabled* have a multitude of talents and abilities that will forever remain untapped, unless they are assisted in their search for meaningful employment in the community.

Below are a few life stories that illustrate the way that person centered planning   can work to connect people with jobs and life roles that are built upon their strengths, talents and dreams for the future.

Affiliation, Admiration and A Dream Job

John, a high school senior, wanted to play football. The special education law required that transition planning for John's move from school to work would take place between the ages of fourteen and twenty-one. When I met John he was just leaving school at the age of about twenty-one. When the topic of employment arose, John would state that he wanted to be a football player. He would not tolerate any other suggestion.

He said he would not work at any other job, and even when he was given another job, he would not work at it.

Between the ages of fourteen and twenty John's job coach had arranged jobs for him. While John could be physically taken to a job, no one could make him work. Upon arrival at the place of employment he would simply walk away from the job or, if pressured to work, he would get down under the table and cover his head.

Many well meaning and kind people tried to help John adjust to the expectations that he would face at work. They explained over and over that when he was taken to a job he must do the job. He must work where he was told to work. When people started trying to help him understand this, he would shout, cover his ears, yell, kick the table, and generally become so unpleasant to be around that he gained the reputation of being a guy that nobody could work with.

So what did they do? They took him to a psychologist. They hoped that there was some medication that would make John docile and willing to sweep the floor in a hospital corridor for the next forty years like he was supposed to.

The doctor asked John why he had come. John knew why they had brought him to see the doctor. He said that he would not work as a janitor because he wanted to play football. The doctor complimented John on not giving up. She told John that he was strong and true to himself by saying what it was that he wanted to do for work, because a lot of people would not have kept trying to communicate when no one would listen to them. John appreciated that the doctor was impressed with his behavior in a good way and his hopes rose a bit.

When John and the doctor talked about John's goal of being a football player they quickly got down to the facts. John's experience with football was that he never missed watching his local team on television. That was his whole experience with football.

The doctor asked hopefully, "How about football at your school? Did you get involved with the high school team at all? Did you work in the locker room or did you go out for the football team? Or did you help out any other team?"

John said, "No, I never had anything to do with sports in school."

Guiding Principle for Planning:
Listen with an open mind. Think creatively. Accept the challenge.

John had no experience with football, per se. What could have made him so determined to be on a football team?

To understand each other we have to listen with our hearts, and listen from an informed and knowledgeable perspective. We need to understand more about why John wants to play football. In listening to John talk about playing football, there was a clear sense of how lonely he was. While at the peak age for team membership he was unaffiliated with any group. John was well aware that people admire football players while he personally felt rejected, alone, vulnerable and inadequate. From John's perspective, membership on the football team would provide him with a blanket of security, a group of people with whom he felt he was welcome and affiliation with a high status group of men. Then he would feel that he was okay. A real man.

So John's goal was socially and developmentally appropriate: he wanted membership in a socially desirable group. Though it may be challenging to help someone meet their personal goal, it is certainly worth a try.

To start the planning process John was asked to make a list of people he liked and trusted. These people were invited to serve, for a period of time, on John's Person-Centered Planning Team. When John's relatives, friends and staff were gathered around the table everyone had a chance to say what was on their mind in regard to the employment plan.

The staff said, "We've done this before, Doctor! John won't do anything but mess around and say he wants to be a football player when everybody can see he can't do that! He's almost twenty-one and he's going to time out for his benefits. If he doesn't go into vocational rehabilitation now there won't be a spot for him later. He has a terrible reputation. We can't even get people to take him on trial, anymore."

John's parents were just beside themselves. They said, "We want him to be happy, but we can't let him time out of services. This must be worked out right now like the experts said!"

The doctor said, "We have tried taking him to a job he said he won't do. It didn't work. Now let's try to work with the interests of the person whose plan this is. John wants to be on a football team. He has stated that he is willing to play any role possible on the team. We need to look into it to see what roles there might be. Let's make a list of people we know who have anything to do with any football team."

Going around the table in a circle, each person (on the hot seat) listed the names of people who they knew who had anything to do with football: the football coach at the high school; a boy on the team at school; a coach for the Parks & Recreation football team; and one person listed a next-door neighbor who was a publicity person for the local NFL team. After a trip or two around the planning team table here were twenty names on the list.

From among those twenty contacts, the planning team needed to help John set up a visit with a team to explore any way that he could affiliate with a team. Each member of the planning team took a name or two to call. The plan was to just explore the idea of "John and football" with people who knew about football teams, to see if anyone would have an idea that might prove to be a first step of some kind. Most of the people on the planning team didn't have much hope for the process, but everyone was willing to give it a try.

When the publicity person for the local NFL team was called and the situation was explained she said, "John can come out for a tour." So he did. What he saw when he got there convinced John that there were several jobs around the football team that he could do; jobs that did not involve catching the ball, carrying the ball, running for the goals and tackling other guys.

John was a model guest during the tour. Everyone liked him. When John explained that he saw some work he could do for the team, the team agreed to let John have an internship in a behind the scenes role: caring for the towels. The job would be to collect towels from anywhere they were dropped, wash and fold them, and count them when they were replaced back on the shelves. John was very excited. He was eager to learn how many towels there were on the shelf. He watched carefully as they demonstrated how to use the washing machine and dryer. He watched carefully to see where the baskets were stored. The main benefit from John's perspective was that he could wear a team jacket. At last, he was a member of the football team. John did so well in his internship that they hired him and he started taking care of the towels as a regular job.

A job with the football team is not a year-round job. John agreed to manage the towels at a local gym during the off-season for football. Just being a member of the team changed everything for John. He became known as "friendly", "helpful", "focused", and "hard working" at both jobs. The last time the doctor saw John's parents they described what happened when they went to the football stadium and saw their son working. One of the football players walked up to the mother and said, "You know, with this guy around here," –and here he gave John a little sock on the arm- "not only does he not loose any towels, you darn well almost don't get to use one at all. He takes it right out of your hands before you have even dried your face." So the team players were teasing him. He fit in. And John had a big happy grin on his face, above his NFL team jacket.

So John actually got to be "on the football team" as he defined it. Person Centered Planning worked out for him. It was a tough process to go through, especially for John's parents who could see that the "clock was ticking away" and that their son was almost out of benefits. They were afraid that if he didn't give in and work as a janitor where the experts had arranged it for him that he would be out, homeless, on the street. Their fear for their son could have led them to refuse to take part in Person Centered Planning, in which case John probably would have been put on psychoactive medication (prescribed drugs) to manage his anxiety and anger; and he may have, actually, ended up on the street.

Have Bag, Will Travel

Mr. Jones is a gentleman who loves to travel. He is ready to go at any time. If a friend called him right now and said, "Hey, Mr. Jones. You want to go to Chicago tonight with me?" He would be packed and ready to go by the time they drove over to his house to pick him up. Mr. Jones wants to go anywhere he can now, because he had not been out of the state institution even once in the thirty years that he lived there.

At the time Mr. Jones was born, people with developmental disabilities like Cerebral Palsy were placed in state institutions as a matter of course. When waves of such people were being reintroduced to the community in the 1980s, Mr. Jones was already middle aged and had never been outside the institution. While he knew from watching television that there was a wide world out there somewhere, there didn't seem to be any way that this gentleman was going to be able to see much of it until he joined the People First self advocacy training group.

At a People First meeting the self advocates engaged in an activity in which they went around the table and spoke about their goals for the coming year. Mr. Jones hesitantly told the group that he wanted to go on a trip. The others in the group asked him where he wanted to go, and he said, "Anywhere!"

> Guiding Principle for Planning:
>
> Things can change.
>
> Just because something hasn't happened yet, it doesn't mean that it can't happen.

Earlier that day his People First Advisor had received a flyer from a conference that was going to take place in Alaska. The flier requested that anyone who wanted to speak at the conference could apply. The advisor met with Mr. Jones the next day and the two decided that they could give a talk about coming out of an institution and having a life in the community. They put together a slide show and pictures and took it to Alaska and where they gave their talk.

After people saw that Mr. Jones could travel so easily, and after Mr. Jones learned how to state his goals, he has had many opportunities to travel. He's now been to New York, Rhode Island, Los Angeles, and Chicago.

It is important for everyone to know that they should never give up trying to get what they want out of life. Sometimes people get worn out. If no one has been listening to them, they can become tired of trying to tell people what they want. Other times people don't have any hope that their dreams really can happen, so they never share their inner-most desires.

But if people who support others can learn to ask, listen, and work towards a goal, it can happen that people's dreams will come true.

The Clothes Model

When Todd was a senior in High School at age twenty his parents took him to see a doctor, because he was having frequent tantrums. The school had recommended behavior therapy so Todd could learn how to follow directions.

Todd was "timing out" of education – meaning that he was almost aged 21 and at that age his free and appropriate public education would end. The school was required to help him transition into employment between the ages of 14 and 21 years, but it was difficult to help Todd find a job because he was considered "difficult to manage".

The job coach working with Todd had developed a good relationship with a retail shoe store chain and he liked to place students in that shop. The chain store would often take on young adults with developmental disability as staff and train them to match shoes in boxes by size, and return the boxed shoes to the shelving by designer and shoe style.

Everyone considered this job to be a great opportunity for a young adult with a developmental disability. Some of the students placed in the shoe store stayed there, matching and shelving shoes for years.

When Todd was taken to the shoe store and told to start learning the ropes, he spent the whole work day punching holes in the walls and throwing boxes of shoes.

The doctor asked Todd, "You don't like working at the shoe store very much, do you?"

Todd said, "No, and I'm not going to." Interestingly, he was right. Todd didn't work at the shoe store. Although, they took him to the shoe store every day and told him to work, he wasn't working. The doctor was impressed by Todd's determination to "not work" at a job he did not want to do. She had the feeling that if there was something Todd did want to do, that he would work very hard until he learned how to do it well. The question was, what did Todd want out of life?

The doctor and Todd talked over a period of a few weeks about what he really wanted to do for a job. He said, "I know what job I want. There is a name for it but I can't remember what it is." Todd could not remember the name of the career, and the doctor, although she tried very hard, could not guess it.

Deciding to take a different track to figure out the missing pieces of the puzzle, the doctor asked Todd to tell her about his hobbies. Todd had a big scrapbook full of pictures of men cut out of magazines and glued onto the otherwise blank pages. Some of the men in the pictures wore suits and were standing by cars; some were shown in restaurants on dates; others were shown sitting at desks in offices. She was not sure why Todd had chosen these particular pictures and was not even sure if the scrapbook was work-related; but she asked him to tell her something about why he chose each specific picture.

Todd eagerly explained, "Well, because of him standing here." As Todd explained in words he stood up and assumed the same stance as the man in the photograph.

The doctor tried again, "I see, the way he is standing. Tell me more."

Todd said, "Well, it's because....see him here? Standing...like this ...by that car? That's what I want to do."

The doctor thought, "He likes the way this guy looks and he wants to wear a suit and stand by a car." No bells were ringing. She was still puzzled about how to help Todd find a job.

Gradually as Todd and the doctor worked their way through the whole scrapbook it dawned on the doctor that the men in the photos were modeling and that Todd wanted to be a model. He wanted to have pictures of himself in magazines.

Guiding Principle for Planning:

There is always a first time! Be a trailblazer when you need to be.

The doctor said, "Let's get a planning team together!"

Todd and his parents made a list. The planning team would consist of his parents, his teachers, a neighbor, one of his dad's old friends, his minister, the doctor, and of course, the leader was Todd. The planning team talked about what they needed to do to help Todd become a model. Todd did not look like a typical model. He had a number of minor and major physical disabilities that simply did not say "typical model". People on the planning team felt that it "wasn't fair" to get Todd's hopes up. Some felt that it was a "fantasy" and that nothing good would come of this type of plan since it was not based on any type of disability related treatment.

It is quite true that modeling can be a difficult business. Most people don't model very long. Among the problems with modeling are that hours are long and the pressure is intense. People have a "look" that goes in and out of style. Sometimes the agency lets a person model for a while, and then their career is over. Todd and the doctor talked about disappointment when you are not the one chosen from an audition and dealing with disappointment in constructive ways. Thinking over all the shoes Todd had thrown in the back of the shoe store (not to mention the holes he punched in walls), he and the doctor talked about how if someone throws even one camera at a modeling show that they will be paying for that camera for the rest of their working life. Todd and the doctor talked about public behavior, grooming and managing conflict. The doctor wanted to be sure that Todd understood that people (those with and those without disabilities) don't always get their own way on the job and every worker has to learn how to accept that.

The doctor explained more to Todd about what the job might be like. She told Todd, "You'll be standing under hot lights for a long, long time and they will say, "Stand still." "Turn this way." Put your hands on your hips."

"You might not want to stand still. They might not say "please or thank you". But Todd was sure it would all go just fine.

By this time in the planning process Todd's mother had paid for a set of professional photographs, a portfolio of Todd in different clothes doing different things in typical model poses, and Todd got an agent. He was signed by the agent one week, and got a call to audition just a week later.

Todd and the doctor had an intense last minute discussion about dealing with disappointment, doing what other people tell one to do, telling people verbally when a person has had enough, and finding a safe place where one could withdraw if needed. This job created a situation in which there was a great potential for blowing up in everybody's face. Everyone was anxious to hear how the first day went. Everyone feared that Todd would fail.

But Todd did so well that the photographer had told his mother he had never had a "more cooperative" model. Todd had never been called "cooperative" before. He had a smile a mile wide when he reported this new part of his reputation to the doctor.

Now Todd models for a clothing catalog. He got the job he wanted and he is doing it successfully. There's no magic to this outcome. He could have had a miserable, unfulfilled and most likely highly medicated life in which he withdrew further and further from those around him. But instead, with his person centered plan Todd had a situation in which somebody listened and said, "Well, let's give this a try, and if it doesn't work we will come back to the drawing board." I

Stick With What You Love

Amie was a girl who loved pizza.

She was at the first stage of career planning, at the age of fourteen years, when she first was introduced to the process of Person Centered Planning. Amie doesn't use spoken language and has been known basically to spend most of her time hiding under the desk at school. She would seldom look at anyone or talk to them, and even her parents described her as very, very withdrawn.

But there is one thing that always made Amie smile, pizza.

Amie really had no other interests besides pizza, that people had been able to observe. If she was taken somewhere she didn't want to go, she would just withdraw. She looked like a paper cut-out of a girl: empty and flat. When she was at home she would withdraw by sitting as still as a statue if she was told that she had to stay in the living room. If allowed to go to her bedroom she would lie stiffly on her bed. Amie's parents brought her to the doctor and they said, "Can you give her some kind of medicine or behavior therapy so that she will participate in life a little more and interact a little more with us? We want her to be happy."

When the doctor tried to talk with Amie she crawled quietly under the desk. The doctor decided that the office probably wasn't a very good place to talk to Amie. So she went to Amie's home. Amie was quiet at home, but she did not object when the doctor was shown into her room. She just sat stiffly and silently, without looking at the doctor. The doctor asked Amie and her parents to name a place where Amie liked to go, and of course, it turned out to be a local restaurant in a chain of pizza store. As soon as they told Amie they were heading out to get pizza, she grew as bright as a button. She hurried to get her jacket and she was the first one out the door on the way to the car. At the restaurant she was animated. She had a huge smile on her face and while she still sat quietly, she was clearly as happy as she could be.

Discussing things with Amie was difficult because she would not participate in person. So the doctor made a short audio tape for Amie to listen to. In the tape the doctor described an idea and then asked a question. Then Amie would take the tape home and listen to it over the week and bring back her answer (yes or no) the next week. By going back and forth over several sessions in this way, Amie was able to say that she wanted to work at the pizza restaurant.

The planning team, consisting of the job coach, a schoolteacher, Amie and her mother and the doctor sat around the table and we created a solid plan that would allow Amie to work at the pizza restaurant. It involved going to school for a half day. Taking the short bus ride from school to the pizza restaurant and working there for three hours. Amie's mother would then pick her up on the way home from her own job. The idea was for a job coach to come with Amie to the job for the first week, and then make periodic visits to the site to assure that Amie was continuing to do the job well. It was a standard plan, like many the job coach had made before. She expected that Amie would do well on the job and she had confidence in the arrangements the planning team had made.

The job coach then took Amie and the plan into the pizza place where the manager said, "I'm not hiring anybody with a disability. Are you kidding? It would gross people out. The rest of my customers would leave. They don't want to see somebody like that here. That's going to drive away my business. Besides, what if she gets hurt? What if she falls down and gets injured? What are my liabilities? Anyway, what could somebody like her do?"

Guiding Principle in Planning:

No one said it would be easy! Keep trying until you get what you want.

The job coach came out of the restaurant in tears. The team met again and came up with a plan of action designed to change the manager's mind about hiring people with disabilities.

The manager remembered that Amie had been coming to eat in the restaurant for years and that she had never done anything disruptive in the store. Of course Amie was so quiet and withdrawn that she had never done anything disruptive, anywhere. The issue, in fact, had always been to try to find ways to get Amie to do anything at all, she was so withdrawn.

The job coach asked the pizza restaurant manager, "Amie comes here to eat quite often. What complaints have you had from your other customers about her? What kinds of things do they not like about Amie when she is here eating?"

The manager had to think a moment, then she said, "Well, actually, the customers all walk over and say, "Hi" to her. So I haven't had any complaints."

The job coach asked if the store carried insurance for their other employees and the manager responded that she was fully covered for each employee, no matter what happened to any employee.

Then the manager just stopped talking for a moment and then she said, "You know what? I see that I have been prejudiced against people with disabilities. I've never realized that before. You've totally opened my eyes. She can come here but she can only stay here if a coach stays with her because I don't have time to watch her and baby her."

So the job coach brought Amie in to work in the pizza restaurant and stayed with her for a week. Now, six years later, Amie has been working at the pizza restaurant full-time since graduation and she is still proud of her job and she still loves pizza. She is proud of the work that she accomplishes every day. She folds boxes for home delivery and piles up boxes higher than her head. She washes the silverware and rolls it up in clean napkins. Amie is working where they sell pizza and on her days off, where do you think Amie wants to go? She wants to go have pizza at the restaurant where she works. The customers go out of their way to go up and talk to her and the whole staff likes her. While it is true that she still isn't talkative, she is very friendly and she is getting along beautifully as a valued member of the team.

In helping someone create a person-centered plan, the name or type of disability is not important. What matters is: 1) the person's interests, 2) their talents and their strengths and 3) the fact that they have some strongly interested people on their planning team who will help them find ways to make their dreams a reality.

Chapter One Thought Questions

After completing the reading of the chapter, read and write an essay answering the following questions:

1. What are the steps of person centered planning?

2. What are the most important aspects of person centered planning?

3. What would you say to a staff member who tells you, "Well, we did a person- centered plan but she still overeats"?

4. Explain how you would go about creating a person-centered employment plan with someone who likes to talk, is helpful, can keep things picked up and likes food.

CHAPTER 2: Navigating the Educational System

A Sign of the Times: Systems in Transition

The next important philosophical and practical step for people who care about people with disabilities is helping people navigate the system that provides them with services and supports. The system is up and running. Everything is in place, but it hasn't been there very long, and we're still learning how to make it work better as we go. As we learn, we revise the system to better meet the needs of the people it serves.

The system is new enough that even through the 1960s, children who had special needs, those who had physical disabilities and cognitive disabilities were not provided with a free or appropriate public education in most cases. There were some isolated situations in which children who had marginal disabilities were allowed to go to preschool or early childhood education or elementary age education, but as they grew older they were generally dropped from the educational system at that time.

The most common approach to education in the 60s was for students with disabilities to be educated in a private school, paid for by parents, or to be institutionalized and educated in self-contained settings, in hospitals, and in treatment centers and institutions. It is still common for those of us working in the field to come across adults in their 50s and 60s who have never been to school and were also never institutionalized. Most of these people lived at home with their parents and stayed home to help their mother with the housework, the gardening, or with caring for the other children.

78

In Chapter 1 I told you about my neighbor, Johnny, and how I was the only child at school who could understand what Johnny said. Johnny lived at home with his family until the age of ten years. He attended the neighborhood school through the third grade, against the loud protestations of his teachers and the parents of his classmates. By the time we were aged ten, after years of being taunted on the playground and ignored in the classroom, Johnny was sent away to an institution to live and to attend school.

Due to confidentiality, I was never allowed to contact him again. He probably came out of the institution when we were in our 40s at the time when social norms called for institutions to be emptied of all possible residents. When Johnny was released back into the community at the age of 40, he returned as a middle aged man to a social setting he had left as a ten year old boy. Imagine all of the life experiences that the rest of us had experienced in the community between the ages of ten and 40, and think of all of the years and opportunities were missing for my friend. It seems impossible for someone to "catch up" under such conditions- and yet all over America people of that generation did just that.

Now times have changed and the social norms call for services and supports to be offered to people with disabilities right in the community where their families live.

Eligibility is the key that unlocks the door to services, and test outcomes are the passport to eligibility for supports.

Every agency that provides services for children or adults has an eligibility guideline and criteria. People are tested by experts in the field, and the test outcomes demonstrate that the person either "meets the criteria" and is eligible for services (if there is not a waiting list), or the test outcomes show that the person "does not meet the eligibility criteria" and will not be given services. It is an "either/ or" situation. In some ways this is an unfortunate situation, because many people who partially meet criteria are in need of the same kinds of supports and services as those who fully meet the criteria. These are the people who fall through the cracks in public services. If their parents can afford to buy private services they will have their needs met, otherwise, they will gradually fall behind despite long years of struggle to keep up with typically developing peers.

The evaluation process itself is very, very lengthy, taking up to six months to complete. A "comprehensive evaluation" will cost somewhere between $3,000 and $10,000; depending upon the types of evaluations that are needed. The more areas of specialization in which an evaluation are needed, the higher the cost will be.

Each area: auditory, genetic, vision, dysmorphology, dental, skeletal, gastroenterology, neurology, and cognitive has its own specialists and its own evaluation process. Each type of evaluation is costly. If a family can not afford the cost or does not have an insurance plan that will pay for the evaluation, then they have the option to request a free evaluation, paid for by the government, from either a "Birth to Three" program offered by their state, or by applying for the insurance provided to children from households that meet the national definition of poverty- often going by the name "Medicaid". Some states also have an Early Childhood program that will do the portions of the evaluation that are needed to set individual educational goals that will impact the child's education.

The evaluation process starts by listening to what the experts think is important, but nothing can take the place of the people closest to this child, and that is their parents. The task of the parents is to take a charge of the situation and find a way to lead their child through the educational process in a way that makes sense to them as a family and in a way that promotes the child's development.

The goal of the family is to maximize the child's potential and help the child learn to set and reach challenging personal goals. Parents need to seek out the experts and listen carefully to what they say. Parents need to have the input of the experts to assure that they are able to offer their child all of the types of help that will be of benefit to the child. But parents should never let the experts take over and plan the child's life. The parents should never lose sight of the fact that they are raising a child, not a client; and that they are raising a child to live a real life, not a program.

81

Working With The Experts

It is critical to maintain excellent records of school reports and medical records in a notebook kept by the parents.

Parents find that they must refer back to old test results and treatments long after they have forgotten the details. It's not easy to get copies of medical records when they are needed, so it is best if the family learns early on to collect all reports and keep them together in a three ring binder notebook.

The notebook will soon become a very valuable reference for the family and it will become critical to the future outcome for the child because tests are repeated on a schedule of two or three years. When the time comes for a child to have a psychological evaluation at the age of two and a half, the specialist will need all of the records about the child from birth onward. When the child has an evaluation done at the age of six, the specialist needs records from the evaluations done at birth; they need records of treatments done between birth and age two; they request results of the evaluation done at age two and a half and all of the records in between. The process of looking backward through the person's developmental history to help chart their course for the future never ends. Throughout the life of the child, professionals will ask questions about the child's development in the early years.

Evaluations are usually re-done by multi- disciplinary teams every third year. Individual evaluations for specific purposes are done annually or when there seems to be a treatment effect that could call for a change in approach. An individual educational plan occurs just once a year at the school with the special education teacher serving as the team leader.

Table 4: Developmental Milestone Evaluations

Age of Child	Common Evaluations Performed
Birth	Physical Evaluation (MDs) Neurological Evaluation Social Work Auditory Physical Therapy
Two to Three Years	Physical Evaluation (MDs) Neurological Evaluation Social Work Auditory Physical Therapy Psychological Evaluation Speech and Language
Three to Thirteen	Physical Evaluation (MDs) Neurological Evaluation Social Work Auditory

	Physical Therapy
	Psychological Evaluation
	Speech and Language
	Educational Achievement
Fourteen to Twenty-One	Physical Evaluation (MDs)
	Neurological Evaluation
	Social Work
	Auditory
	Physical Therapy
	Psychological Evaluation
	Speech and Language
	Educational Achievement
	Employment (Transition) Planning

While doctor offices keep records for some years, the family's records need to be complete and comprehensive because signing releases and waiting for medical record copies is a very time consuming and lengthy process.

Families should also keep a series of home evaluations that they perform for their child. Parents should make it their business to learn the normal ranges for developmental milestones, and consistently monitor the child's growth and performance. Parents should learn the developmental stages and then take the time to observe their child on a routine basis so that they can monitor the child's progress. In the early months when development occurs rapidly, parents should take time to write down each new sound, word, motion and ability or skill that the child develops on a chart that notes the child's age at the time the skill developed.

Monitoring a child's progress is not to be done for the purpose of putting pressure on the child to develop faster than they are already developing (which would never work, anyway), but to maintain a clear record of events that will help the family understand how their child learns and how to help the child maximize their potential.

Keeping school-work samples, drawings the child has done, finger-paintings the child has made, and later, writing samples, in the notebook is important, as well. Keeping the notebook up-to-date with every new evaluation and every new report is in the best interest of the child because the time is going to come when someone will need to know the age of the child when a particular skill developed. If the team can just flip open the book and find the information there, the child will be able to get the help they need, when they need it, because nothing's been lost, misplaced, or can't be found. I have seen many instances in which the doctor has gone out of practice, or the staff at the specialist's office says the report needs to be regenerated. In some cases the information that is considered critical by the new evaluator is simply lost forever.

American law entitles a child to a "free" and "appropriate" education. As you can imagine, getting general agreement on what a "free and appropriate educational setting" actually is becomes part of the problem. By "free" the government means that the family doesn't have to pay for it. (I don't think there is usually any question about that.) But defining the word <u>appropriate</u> is a problem because the setting some people would think was appropriate for any specific child would be in the institution for a certain child, whereas others would disagree and say, "No, they should be in their neighborhood classroom." Still others would look at the same child and say, "Well they can go to the regular school district, but they have to go to a self-contained classroom with only other people like themselves." And frequently I even hear this comment, "They'd be happier if they were off with others like themselves. They can't compete with the normal children, so they're not going to be happy in a normal setting."

Right now developing social norms in our country call for something known as "inclusion". Inclusion is the placement of a child in the same classroom in which she or he would be placed if they did not have a disability. Inclusion is based upon a belief that children are thought to be best served in inclusive (everybody welcome) settings in which they learn and play with others of their age group, both with and without disabilities. Parents need to make it their task to find out what the options are for their child and as they enter the planning process they must "dream big" for their child.

Dream Big

The parent of the child is the ultimate expert on the child, and upon parents falls the ultimate responsibility for the child's development. When the experts and the teachers have faded into the distant past, the parents

86

are still there, working tirelessly to help their child succeed in life.

Many parents depend upon teachers, therapists, and other specialists to help them decide what is best for their child. The team approach is a good one, because it helps to assure that all options have been discussed and that the resulting plan is one that will help the child maximize their talents and abilities.

It is in the best interest of the child for the parents of the student with the disability and the teachers of the student with the disability learn how to work together early in the child's school life.

I know of one case in which the child involved had a progressive disease that gradually weakened the child to the point that by the time he was in late grade school he was on life support. He had the kind of wheel chair that laid down, so he was laying down flat, and he had a breathing machine and another machine that had to be on at all times. He had attended the same school throughout his childhood wanted to come to the classroom and be with his peers and continue learning. The parents fought hard for the right to send him to school with his peers (and the school fought just as hard to keep him out). Eventually the courts decided that the burden on the school was too heavy, and he was kept out of school for the last two years of his life. When he died the boy's parents were enraged to receive a set of sympathy notes that a teacher had the children write – the same children with whom he should have attended school, but whom he had not seen for the last two lonely years of his life.

There was another case in which a little boy in the second grade who had a gastroenterological disability was still soiling himself (that is, having bowel movements in his clothes instead of in the bathroom) was prohibited from attending school until that situation was resolved. He was out of school for two years, returning to the classroom when he was in the fourth grade.

Both sets of parents took their fight to court; and both children lost. In both cases so much time went by that the lives of the children involved were impacted most of all simply by losing the right to live as normal a life as was possible during the critical years of their childhood.

Everyone understands why the school did not want these children with disabilities to attend. It would have been a lot of work for the school. However, the children were not well served by isolation and rejection. The most important thing is for all of the adults involved to work together to find the best solution- one that would best serve the social, academic, medical and special needs of the children. Surely there was some way to make sure that no child is kept out of school for medical reasons.

Giving It "All You Got!"

Paul was born with a portion of his brain that was not enervated (there were no nerves and no blood veins). This area extended into both hemispheres of the brain and in three lobes. His challenges were in articulation, gross and fine motor (writing and movement), and in specific learning disabilities (math, spelling). Worst of all, from the perspective of the teacher, he could not sit still and keep his hands to himself. Since he had above average intelligence and a wide array of knowledge, and was very handsome, it appeared to teachers that he was just naughty.

Paul was expelled from preschool and Kindergarten. He was held back in the first grade. Classmate's parents asked plaintively (in his hearing) why they had to have a 'retard' in their class. The teacher complained to Paul's parents that she never wanted to go into Special Education and said that she resented having to have a 'disabled kid' in her class.

Paul's mother was a teacher, also. She knew that acceptance among peers and attending school were important for Paul's future as an adult. She was determined to make the situation work.

The school wanted to place Paul in a segregated setting, a classroom far away from the 'normal children'. They said that the Special Education teachers were specially trained to help children 'like Paul' and that segregation would be the most appropriate setting for him.

Paul's parents talked the school into letting them serve as unpaid classroom volunteers in Paul's classroom. The school agreed, thinking that the parents would soon tire of it so they could then relegate Paul to the segregated classroom. But Paul's mother faithfully attended class with  Paul until he graduated from High School at age 19. Since some specific teachers (like the biology teacher in high school) refused to have him in the class. For those classes that the public school refused to offer, Paul's mother purchased home-study coursework for Paul that they worked on together at home. Paul's mother worked almost full time, as well. Paul's mother and father collaborated in timing their work schedules so that one parent was always home while the other parent worked.

His family knew that Paul needed help to make a good social adjustment. During all these years Paul's mother and father served as a boy scout leader, and the soccer team mom, and worked very hard among the other mothers to help Paul gain acceptance among peers.

Through extreme diligence and artful planning and some good luck, Paul was able to complete high school. He earned a perfect score on the ACT and went to a competitive college. However, since he had never been able to receive the help he needed from faculty and staff at school, he was unable to make the mental leap required to accept help from the faculty in college. He simply did not turn in his work, and his college career lasted only one year.

Paul is now thirty. He went on to a career in construction. He reads history, geography and anthropology in his spare time, and designs and builds racing bicycles. While he is functioning as an adult in the world (which is great) he continues to feel that he failed in some important way, and to wish that he had been able to succeed in college.

Navigating the Special Education System

As you see from Paul's story, the educational laws and current practices may either support a person with a disability in getting an education or sometimes limit their full participation. This chapter will explore the ways in which the Individuals with Disabilities Education Act (IDEA) empowers parents and teachers to advocate for children with disabilities.

In 1975 the United States Congress passed a law covering the education of children with a disability4. The law has been ratified (or re-approved) every five years since that time, most recently in 2004. The major advantage of the IDEA legislation is that after its passage all public schools are required to provide every school-aged child with a free and appropriate education. IDEA requires that children with the following disabilities are covered in the act:

1. Autism
2. Mental Retardation
3. Hearing Impairments
4. Deafness
5. Visual Impairments
6. Speech or Language Impairments
7. Serious Emotional Disturbances
8. Orthopedic Impairments
9. Traumatic Brain Injury
10. Specific Learning Disabilities
11. Other Health Impairments

Special Education is defined in the law this way: *Special education is designed instruction that meets the unique needs of a child with a disability.*

---

[4] http://idea.ed.gov/

Below are the six major areas in which IDEA impacts the education of children:

1. All Children Must Be Served By the Public School

It was the intention of Congress that all children would be served in their local public schools. All states must provide services for children from birth through the age of eighteen years, and most states provide services from birth through twenty-one.

2. Children will be assessed to determine need.

Before children can enter special education they must have an interdisciplinary evaluation to determine both their strengths and weaknesses. In order to assure that the tests are unbiased, they must be given in the native language of the child and in such a way that their abilities and disabilities are accurately displayed. Children may never be placed in special education based on their performance on a singular examination and the reports of all of the professionals must be considered in the final placement decision.

3. Each child is guaranteed a free (no cost) public education that is designed appropriately to meet their unique learning needs.

The "appropriateness" of each educational plan can not be determined by one person, but must be arrived at through discussion by a committee of educational specialists, disability specialists and the parents.

This plan is called the Individual Educational Plan (IEP). http://www.ed.gov/parents/needs/speced/iepguide/index.html

In children younger than the age for preschool (usually age three years) the law allows for the Department of Mental Health and Developmental Disabilities to work with a similar committee to develop an Individualized Family Service Plan (IFSP). http://www.ldaamerica.org/aboutld/professionals/guidelines.asp

4. Children with and without disabilities are educated together

Before IDEA most children with special needs were segregated away from children who were developing typically. However, IDEA guarantees students the right to be educated in "the least restrictive environment" which means that the school must educate the children together except for the smallest possible amount of time in which the child with the disability must be educated separately or individually in order to meet their own specific needs.

5. Parents are an important part of the IEP process and can challenge the decision made by the team, when they believe it is not in the best interest of their child.

Prior to the IDEA parents who did not agree with the decisions made by the school had no recourse to a review process to challenge that decision. After IDEA came into law parents and students have a right to "Due Process" or a legal process of professional review by an impartial third party.

6. Parents have the right of signature

In addition to the right to be a part of the decision making process for their child's education, parents have the basis right to serve as the final authority on the plan, through their signature. Despite these precautions, most parents initially feel overwhelmed and unsure about how to advocate for their child through the process, especially if they disagree with any of the professional assessment findings. There are parent websites and books that help parents as they find ways to support their child's best interests throughout childhood. [See Disability Accommodations Handbook, Whitehead 2007].

Procedures and Partners

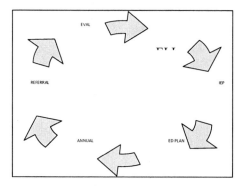

Figure 1: IEP Process

As shown in the diagram based upon the book, *Negotiating the Special Education Maze* (Anderson, Chitwood, Hayden, 1997), the school IEP process begins with a referral from the classroom teacher. Sometimes the parent has asked the classroom teacher to make a referral and other times the classroom teacher is the person who first decides that the child probably has a delay and needs an evaluation. The teacher sends the referral to the Principal who convenes a committee to determine if an evaluation should take place. Parents must sign agreement for the evaluation process to begin. After the comprehensive evaluation is done, using professionals from all relevant fields of specialization the entire group convenes and writes an individual educational plan. The plan is put in place and carried out by the classroom teacher and all specialty teachers needed, such as a reading instructor. After each 12 month period the child's progress is reviewed, the plan is reviewed and a referral for a re-evaluation is submitted by the classroom teacher or the special education case manager for a re-evaluation. The major evaluation involving all professions is done once every third year.

Parents are Key

Starting early in the child's life, the parents need to learn how to observe their child in a systematic way. This is good thing for any family to do, but it is critical when the child has an <u>atypical developmental pattern</u>. It's very hard to achieve the necessary level of objectivity in observing one's own child because parents identify so strongly with their children and they want for their child to succeed. It can be very hard for parents to let go of their own background and experiences, the hopes and dreams they had for themselves which parents often project onto their children. But parents must learn to apply scientific observation in a systematic way to the child so that they can determine what the child's current level of performance is, what the goal for the child is, and what the child needs from teachers, assistants, friends and parents in order to assure the child's future success. Parents are the key to the child's success. Below is an interesting website for parents: http://www.taalliance.org/centers/index.htm

A Circle of Friends

While parents need to know who the key people are to interact with and support their child through his or her educational process and it is critical that knowledgeable experts are involved, because it really does take a village to raise a child.

An enriched childhood can not be accomplished without the heartfelt, very caring input of family members, friends of family, and others in the community that have an interest. One of the most useful tools developed in the 1990's is called a circle of friends. A circle of friends is a carefully selected group of people of all ages that care about the child and who will remain constant "cheerleaders" from the time a child is born through out their life. Early in the child's life the parents identify other children in the community of the same age who would be age-mates to the child, and they set up a playgroup, which starts very, very young, they invite key relatives, adult friends, religious leaders and neighbors to join the circle. This circle helps think through all of the difficult issues that arise in the child's life which helps the parents. They are consistent forces of "acceptance" and "friendliness" for the child, which helps counteract the many thoughtless and cruel ways others may treat the child.

The circle of friends helps the child with social development, self-concept and self-identity of the person. It's very important that some of the people in the circle of friends are approximately the same age as the child for whom the plan is being developed. That will keep the plan appropriate and ensure that it's a contemporary living plan that grows and changes as would be appropriate for anyone of that age. The website below will provide more information for the interested reader.

http://www.inclusive-solutions.com/circlesoffriends.asp

Individual Educational Plan

The evaluation process leading to the IEP will define the child's development in several developmental areas. These are: Movement, Communication, Social Relationships, Self-Concept/ Independence, Senses/ Perception, and Cognitive Skills. We will discuss each term below.

Movement

Movement is the ability to walk, climb stairs, run, jump (the gross motor skills), sit in a chair, sit at a desk, write, hold objects (fine motor skills), chew and swallow food and keep one's balance when "ambulating" or walking.

Communication

Communication is the ability to understand (called <u>receptive language</u>) when someone tries to communicate with one through language, whether spoken language or sign, written symbols or letters, and / or facial expression. It is also the ability to express one's own meaning clearly by any of these types of communication, which is called <u>expressive language</u>.

Social Relationships

Social relationships are the ability to relate to others. This developmental area can be observed through watching a person engage in play or shared work. One part of the developmental area is related to the ability to develop meaningful relationships with peers (as friends) and the other part relates to the ability to identify with and love family members or a significant other as appropriate to the child's age.

Self Concept / Independence

The self-concept area relates to the ability to distinguish one's self as a unique and individual person. Self care (often called <u>self-help skills</u>) is often described in this area, with the ability to eat on one's own, dress one's self and use the bathroom independently.

Senses / Perception

Sensory evaluations focus on the ability to see, hear, smell, taste and use touch to learn about the environment.

Cognitive Skills

Cognitive skills relate to the ability to think, reason, and solve problems. As a person grows older they are expected to demonstrate ability to make associations between dissimilar things, to classify things by groups, to understand similarities and differences, and to comprehend cause-and-effect relationships. School skills such as reading, arithmetic and spelling are clustered in this area during the school years, as well.

The parent and the child's advocate should learn how to observe the child's progress in each of these areas, since the same broad areas are the categories that the school will use to determine which specialists need to be involved in the Individual Educational Plan for the child and which do not.

The IEP meeting, then, is critical to the child's success. What is the role of the parent? Parents and advocates need to be clear on what their role is before they even walk in the door. Understand what the law has provided for schools to do. Understand what the state department of health provides for and what they do not, understand what the school district rules and regulations are. Play your role to its fullest for the benefit of your child or the child for whom you are advocating. Know ahead of time what you need others to do and hold them to it.

An advocate went to an IEP meeting for a high school boy who was a 10th grader, and he had been placed in a regular physical education class because the school did not have an Adaptive PE class for students with special needs. He was lumped in with the other students without special needs in the class. The PE teacher and his assistant (who was still in school and doing his training) did not like having a student in the class that had special needs.

The PE teacher and his assistant came to the IEP with a huge notebook full of example after example of everything this child had done wrong in the class. They had listed every time the child didn't follow directions, every time the child went left instead of right, every time the child did each different thing, such as coming in late from changing or running around with shoelaces dangling. They brought up each incidence as a reason why the child should be punished or failed and removed from the course. As the child's advocate The advocate said to them, "I think you've done a great job of documenting what the need is. You have documented very successfully the need of this child for an Adaptive Physical Education class. What is your plan now to establish that accommodation for him?" They were just stunned because they did not even think about what to do, they were documenting the problems in hopes of getting rid of the child. In the end, the principal took the perspective of the doctor and the PE teacher was put on probation. He could not return to the classroom until he had earned graduate credits over the summer in accommodating special education students in his courses.

It's critical that you know what your child or the child for whom you are advocating needs from the school. If no one advocates for the child, that child will simply not get what they need, because most classroom teachers do not understand how to help children with special needs.

Over and over again, I've had a teacher say to me in the IEP meeting (just like Paul's teacher), "I didn't want to teach Special Ed. I didn't go into Special Ed because I don't like it. Now just look! I've got Special Ed kids all over my classroom now. It's too much work and I don't know how to do it. I don't even want to know how to do it. I want this kid out of my class." Without an advocate most children will drop out of school, because it is very difficult to face this kind of attitude towards you, every day.

School Records and Reports

Parents should have a three-ring binder at home in which they keep all of the records pertaining to their child over the years. As each school letter, recommendation or report is sent home, it should be quickly added to the binder, because it will be needed at some later time to aid in future decision making. Samples of the child's academic "seat work" should also be kept to illustrate the advances the child is making as they grow.

Reporting Progress To Parents

The IEP must provide a statement of how the student's parents will be regularly informed of their child's progress toward the annual goals and the extent to which that progress is sufficient to enable the student to achieve the goals by the end of the year. The frequency at which parents are informed must be at least as often as parents of students without disabilities are informed of their child's progress.

The method or combination of methods to inform the parents of their child's progress may be determined by each school. The schools can decide to make formal reports in the same manner to each student with an IEP, or they may decide that different methods are more effective for some situations.

Among the methods that can be used to inform parents of their child's academic progress are the following: parent-teacher conferences, written progress reports and student-parent-teacher conferences. The reports to the parent do not need to be lengthy or even to contain specific information, but they must meet the conditions explained above. For example, the report to parents must include a statement of the goals with a written report of where the student is currently functioning in that goal area and/or a rating of progress to indicate whether the student's progress to date will likely result in the student reaching the goal by the end of the year. For example, let's take the case of Johnny, who is interested in science and sea life, this year.

> **Annual Goal: [Typical Goal]** "Johnny will use graphic organizers to write a three-paragraph essay using correct sequencing of sentences including topic sentence, supporting sentences and conclusion."
>
> **[Improved Goal written with Johnny's preferences at the center]** "Johnny will study Whales (his choice) and produce a written report of three paragraphs using correct sequencing of sentences including a topic sentence, supporting sentences and conclusion by [date]. He will be supported in this effort by [name] and [name]. He will watch 1 documentary film on whales, read one magazine article, and read one book as resources for his project."

Figure 2: Sample Annual Goal

It is easy to see that the student who participates fully in designing learning goals will understand the goal, become excited about the goal, work faithfully toward achieving it and will be proud of his progress.

Table 5: Johnny's Report on IEP Progress

> Period 1: November
> Johnny watched his film, read his magazine and book about whales and is writing sentences without correct sequencing.
>
> Period 2: January
> Johnny is writing three-sentence paragraphs with correct sequencing, including a topic sentence, supporting sentence and conclusion.

Objective met.

Period 3: March Johnny needs assistance to develop the outline, but once developed, he follows it to accurately write a five-sentence paragraph using a graphic organizer. He is writing two-paragraph essays when following a written outline when provided. Objective not met.

Period 4: June Johnny independently develops a graphic organizer (outline) and writes multiple five- sentence paragraphs using correct sequencing of sentences. Objective Met.

July – August Next meeting to set goals for coming semester.

Disagreements and Due Process

When disagreements concerning a child's support in reaching set learning goals or in setting new learning goals arise, parents should first contact the classroom teacher in writing, then the head of the committee on the IEP document. If the ensuing discussion can not resolve the problem, the law provides for parents to be able to require an impartial third party to review the situation and make a determination in regard to the disagreement.

Placement decisions are the area of greatest conflict between schools and families. Most schools expect children to be included in the regular classroom most of the day and it is most often the case that schools arrange what are called "pullouts" in which a child is taken to a smaller room down the hall from the regular classroom for a short special education in reading, writing, and math. But in some locations there are still schools where children are completely kept in self-contained classrooms and these parents file Due Process requests.

Punishment is another area in which the law protects children with special needs because so many children with an IEP are not able to understand as quickly and as fully as other students what would constitute a punishable behavior. These children are protected under the law, but the school is also protected under law, and after a certain number of trial and errors a child who does not follow the rules will not allowed to attend school in either an open setting or an inclusive setting, any longer. It is critical for child advocates to know what the standards are and to work very, very, very tirelessly with the child **ahead of time** to prevent anything from happening which would result in the child losing their privilege or their right to attending an inclusive setting.

Monitoring is the key

Everyone monitors the child at the school. Teachers are monitoring. The administration is monitoring. The state is monitoring, and those parents had better be monitoring their child as well. It's critical to keep up-to-date with everything. It takes a lot of time and a lot of energy, and people have to really put their heart into it, but monitoring and keeping current on what's happening is the only way to protect the child from losing their civil rights and losing their ability to be included.

The Autism Law network provides the following information :

"There are common issues that arise in due process cases. The most common issues are whether the school district failed to provide a free appropriate public education (FAPE) and/or committed serious procedural violations that resulted in a denial of a free appropriate public education to your child or a denial of parent participation in the IEP process.

If you are considering filing for due process, you should seek the advice of a special education attorney. There is little chance you will prevail in a due process hearing unless an experienced special education attorney represents you, or perhaps a top-notch advocate who has a history of successful due process cases. The only exception might be if there is a single uncomplicated issue, such as the failure of the school district to respond to a request for prior written notice. Even then, you should consult with a special education attorney before filing for due process.

Due Process Checklist

Do you have a complete copy of your child's school file?

If the school is offering a placement and/or services that you do not believe is appropriate, you need to find out as much information as possible about the offered placement and services. Have you made "Prior Written Notice" requests to obtain information about the offered placement and services? (See front page article on the this website, Section - Prior Written Notice)

Do you have a qualified expert witness who has assessed your child and will be able to testify on behalf of your child? Most cases center on whether your child has been denied a free appropriate education?

If this is the case in your due process, you will likely need an expert witness who has assessed your child, written a report and can testify as to the following issues:

1. A description of the tests performed, history taken, observations.

2. A description of your child's disability.

3. How this disability adversely affects your child's education.

4. A description of your child's unique needs (academic, social, adaptive living skills).

5. Whether the school's goals and objectives were appropriate.

6. A description of the appropriate teaching methods, the placement, the specific program and services that are appropriate - with recommended days and hours, qualifications of personnel, classroom environment.

7. If you are contending that the school's placement and services are not appropriate, the expert's reasons therefore.

8. If you are seeking a private placement or services, the reasons that the expert believes the private placement and or services are appropriate.

9. If you are claiming that the placement and services the school has been providing are not appropriate, you will likely need an expert to testify that your child has not made reasonable educational progress. What proof do you have to show that your child was not afforded with

a free appropriate public education? Do you have a record of testing? Samples of your child's work?

If the school is offering a new program that you do not believe is appropriate, you will most likely need an expert to testify that the new program and services will not allow your child to make educational progress. Have you been able to have your expert observe the placement offered by the school?

If you do not have an expert, have you considered requesting a free Independent Educational Evaluation?"

Reference <u>Autism Law</u> July 31, 2007

http://www.aboutautismlaw.com/are_you_ready_to_file_for_due_proc ess.html

IEP Specifics for Accommodating Students With Special Needs

Both adults and children with disabilities have protection under Public Law 504, which is known as "Other Health Impaired" http://4.17.143.133/index.cfm . Relevant diagnoses fit within the categories described below.

As we discussed earlier there are several categories of disability that are covered in the legislation. These specific diagnoses can be clumped together in five areas of need for specific educational accommodation.

The five accommodation categories are:

1. Students with specific cognitive or academic difficulties

2. Students with social or behavioral problems

3. Students with general delays in cognitive and social functioning

4. Students with physical or sensory challenges

5. Students with advanced cognitive development

These categories were created to cover most of the types of accommodation that a student might need to have in a classroom setting and, of course, a number of specific diagnoses fit under each one of the accommodation categories. We will discuss each one below.

Cognitive or Academic Difficulties

When a child is said to have a specific cognitive or academic disability it means that the child has been tested and has an intelligence quotient that falls "in the normal range". That is: the person has been given an Intelligence Test and the findings were in the average or above average IQ range, but they don't do as well in school as would be expected given their normal range intelligence.

Children and adults fit this category when their academic performance is two standard deviations below average in reading, math, or some other academic area such as handwriting. Children in this category would be given an individual educational plan in a specific learning disability.

Characteristics of children within this category are that a child with a learning disability has gaps or holes in their knowledge base. While they may be years ahead in some academic areas, such as science or reading, they will be years behind in another, such as math or handwriting. In this group of children we anticipate that there will be occasional, unusual, and very inappropriate interpretations of what they hear, so their behaviors will be shockingly out of line, surprisingly out of line given that they're generally speaking quite a bright person.

Here's one example: Timothy, a young man in his 20s had been diagnosed at the age of 7 with a specific learning disability in writing called dysgraphia and another specific learning disability in math called dyscalculia and he had a speech delay. The young man was as sharp as a tack in conversation and people were quite impressed with his general knowledge base. This was a  very bright young man who went to college and afterward started his own business, as can many students with developmental delays and learning disabilities who reach parity with their peers in their adult lives.

But one day this well educated young man noticed that the water purifier on his parents' kitchen sink was reading in the red range. The filter is green when the charcoal filter is still fresh, and the water coming through has been filtered. It turns red to let you know the charcoal filter has been exhausted, and it's time to change to a new filter. When he saw the filter was reading in the red range Timothy knew that it meant the filter was no longer working. It needed to be changed. To him that meant that his parents would have to spend the five dollars a new filter would cost. He is so bright and so good with his hands that he figured out a way to reset the filter so that it read green again, despite the fact that it really should have been reading red because it was no longer working. He showed a lack in judgment, because instead of thinking, "Oh, now it's not going to purify the water any more. We don't want to drink that water." He was thinking, "I fooled it. It started to show red. It was telling us we had to spend money on a new filter, and I saved the day and made it show green again."

This is one of the persistent problems that a specific learning disability causes a person: it makes the person fail to consider all aspects of a problem. A learning disability can make even a bright person take action without a full understanding of all of the issues, and without planning ahead.

People can learn to overcome this type of natural consequence of a disability. What is a suggested classroom strategy that could be of some help to students with Learning Disabilities (or specific cognitive and academic difficulties?)

The teacher would need to determine the child's prior knowledge about each new topic and remind them of what they do know about the topic prior to telling them anything new. The teacher needs to "fire up" a student with a learning disability and help set the stage for them so that they ask questions about the new information they don't understand.

Going back to the learning situation with the water coming out of the faucet, Timothy had to be asked to consider "Why do you think the family wanted to filter water to begin with? (Answer: So that they could drink purified water.)

Then Timothy could be asked to consider "Why would the light sometimes be green and then turn red? (Answer: It is green when the purifier is working and red when the purifier stops working.)

Then Timothy is asked , "Would that be a good thing, then, to fool the water filter or would the needs of the family be better served by replacing the water filter even if it costs a few dollars?"

After receiving help in thinking through things that he has not initially considered, Timothy can learn an awareness that there is more than meets the eye in many situation. He can be nudged to look deeper before taking action. That's the kind of exploration of events, the type of learning strategy that's needed all the way through school for a person with a learning disability, and beyond into adulthood.

The student's comprehension of the spoken word and the written word would also need to be carefully, carefully monitored because of misinterpretation that is so common with a learning disability. People with a learning disability need to constantly remember to look for an alternative interpretation of whatever they see happening around them. They can't just go with their first impulse, something most people with LD have trouble learning. They have to learn to stop, reflect, review what they know, and ask themselves further questions so they know where to go.

Why have the schools clustered disabilities into various categories? There are some advantages of categorizing. For one thing, students in the same category have some characteristics in common, so they may benefit from the same instructional or accommodation strategies. This would allow the teacher to use best practices for areas of special need that came out of a research setting.

Another advantage of categorizing is that categories provide a rallying point around which social and political forces can promote the special interest of students. Parents, teachers and student advocates have effected wide policy change in disability education rights and employment rights. There have been torts and class action suits that to support the rights of students over all, as well as by accommodation category.

Finally, it's also an advantage because funding, federal funding comes based on categories. For example, the United States Department of

Education has a program to fund technical assistance for blind people; another to fund programs and technical assistance for deaf people and other specifically designed to serve people with mental retardation. Therefore obtaining a specific U.S. classification qualifies students for federal funding made available for their specific disability. The implication for the teacher is that the teacher has to use the label of

There are also times in which a label is a distinct disadvantage for the persons' labeled. For one thing, there can be disagreement about what specific category a person belongs. Even the experts disagree about the definitions of some categories. Psychologists sometimes do testing for "differential diagnosis" in which they search for evidence to support the inclusion of a person in a specific category, or in more than one category if there are an overlap of symptoms. The implication for the teacher and the student advocate is that they must have some level of sophistication and awareness that labels mean different things to different people. People are sometimes placed in one category when they really could have as well been in another.

Within the field there is also disagreement about identification procedures. Experts disagree about how to identify members of categories, and it is quite true that different procedures sometimes lead to different conclusions about which students have special needs. In many cases a student will be in a special needs category for a few years, and then a question arises about the appropriateness of the inclusion in that category and one or another of the team members want to deny the student inclusion in a specific category. Sometimes parents have been trying to get the child into special education for years, and the school does not allow them the entree'. That most often happens when the diagnosis in question is a learning disability. Both the teacher and the student's advocate need to use multiple and varied sources of information in assessing special needs in students and look for a consistent pattern in the information obtained through testing and observation.

This is a difficult task for the teacher. Teachers report that it is an enormous burden to concentrate intellectually on one student out of many in the class. They feel the stress of observing and like a detective, trying to figure out what sense can be made out of what the child is; what patterns those behaviors fall into. This is one of the important reasons that all parents should have a three ring binder notebook on their child. The parents need to learn about disability and they should also be watching the test outcomes and their child's behavior so that they can discern for these patterns that lead to diagnosis and inclusion in a special needs category. By collecting objective data about their own student they can assist the teacher in this very difficult task of truly trying to be a detective; and figure out the global meaning of individual actions and behaviors.

Looking for a pattern takes a lot of energy, and a lot of time, and yet it's the only way to assure that a student will be able to get what they need.

We have discussed the ways in which there is heterogeneity (that is "sameness") within each category. However, it must be remembered that members of the category are also very different from each other in important ways. To use just one of the categories – sensory disability- just because people in the category share the characteristic that they are blind they do not necessarily share any other characteristics. The diagnosis of "blind" does not identify anything about the person's cognitive ability, their interests, their preferences, their motivation, their hopes and dreams and goals, and how they'll eventually end up making use of their lives. The category itself just shows that they're facing similar barriers in sensory input and that similar accommodations may be of use to them.

People mistake the breadth of the category many times, and believe that it provides more extensive information than it really does. Many times teachers, employers and others call the psychologist and ask, "What kind of job can a deaf person do? What kind of job can a retarded person do?"

In the first place, we're talking about people with disabilities.

We put the person first. *Never* call someone a "disabled" person. They are spoken of as a person with a disability.

The only answer is that people are differentially talented and have many different interests, hopes and dreams. There is no particular job would suit everyone with any special need. People with special needs are as different, and as unique in their talents and their preferences as are people without disabilities. For this reason instructional methods need to be tailored to individual students, although the category gives the teacher a "starting place" and a way to assure that she or he is using best practices for the field. It must be clear, however, that the teacher cannot assume that any particular method would be equally suitable for all members of the category.

Finally, a label is stigmatizing. Labels communicate inferiority. Labels communicate inadequacy. In fact "invalid" means invalid. People are badly hurt by labels. It became popular in the 1990's to refer to students in special education no longer as retarded or as brain damaged, but to call them "developmentally delayed." Then, on the playground, instead of taunting "you're a retard"; now a cruel child will point at another child and taunt, "You're developmental! You're developmental!"

We're all developmental, since "developmental" means that we are all learning and growing and developing at all times. Children don't know the meaning of the word, they just know it means something bad. They know the adults think the child is inferior to them. The label brands the person inferior in some important way.

So whenever possible, it's important to not use labels. It's often unnecessary to even refer to the special need when you're talking about someone. For example, if I had a classroom speaker coming, I would not necessarily say, "I'm having a person with a disability come to talk to you." I would say, "I'm having a person who's an expert in accommodations come to talk to you." You see what I mean? Avoid the label wherever possible because the label stigmatizes the person, diminishes them, and actually hurts them the same way it would hurt you if it were applied to you.

Always, *always*, <u>always</u>, **always** use people first language when talking about people. It's a person with a disability, not a disabled person. In fact, many people with disabilities really don't like the word "handicapped" because handicapped comes from the time back a century or so when people with disabilities were forced to beg. They stood with their cap in their hand and begged for money in their cap. So it's a hurtful label to many people. It's important to avoid using labels whenever possible.

Below is a chart showing the five categories used in schools, with the characteristics of the students in each category and a description of how the teacher can accommodate the child in the classroom.[5]

---

[5] Ormrod, J. (2003). Educational Psychology. Merrill Prentice Hall: New Jersey

Instructional Categories For Accommodations

Category 1: Cognitive, Specific Learning Disabilities

Timothy:

Timothy loves the social aspect of school and would tell you that recess is his favorite subject. He has trouble with reading and/or math, but he excels in science, art, woodworking and P.E. The other boys like him because he is fearless and takes risks. He is loud and restless and finds it hard to sit still. Everything he has is broken or he has lost it again. He runs outside without his coat and hat, and doesn't seem to notice that he is wet to the skin when it rains. He is very interested in what the teacher has to say, loves television and computers, plays computer games well but he finds it very hard to stay focused on his seat work and he seldom hands in an assignment. If he has understanding parents he is generally good natured and playful. If he lives with criticism he may be rude and aggressive.

Students included in this category have a different learning style although their intelligence is average or above. What works for other students will not necessarily work for them. They have a unique, individual learning style that must be accommodated, for if learning is to take place. Their academic progress is much more uneven than is usual among students with IQ in the average range. On the one hand some students with learning disabilities read five or six grade levels above their own grade level, and yet their performance in math or in handwriting will be four years delayed from their grade level. This type of presentation is very, very common. Such a student may fail to understand what is said to them, will often be inappropriate socially (such as acting younger than their age sometimes, or being unusually noisy and disruptive at other times). Sometimes while students in this category learn more slowly in their area of disability, they have areas of great advanced learning as well.

Table 6: Learning Disability

Category 1: Learning Disability
Anticipated Characteristics of Students: Uneven pattern of development Difficulty remembering <ul><li>Poor listening</li><li>Poor reading & math skills</li><li>Difficulty getting home work done</li><li>Forgetting to turn in homework</li><li>Forgetting previously learned material</li></ul>
Best Practices for Instruction: Set individual objectives with the student not for the student <ul><li>Break the task down into steps and explain ho to do one step at a time</li><li>Use computer tools to compensate for areas of weakness</li><li>Support the student when doing lessons and homework to</li></ul>

provide ongoing feedback and encouragement

- Have the student teach the material to someone else

Category 2: Social and/or Behavioral Problems

Mary:

Mary was diagnosed with a severe emotional disturbance when she was five-years old. Mary had not spoken a word since she was three. When the therapist started working with her she was in her second foster home. She had been removed from the custody of her family following a situation in which her father killed her mother in front of her. The father had been incarcerated and since the mother had died, she was put in a foster home.

Mary would not speak, did not respond to being spoken to, and her silence created such friction for the first foster family that they just moved her on. The second foster family brought her in to see a therapist. The child had not spoken a word in a couple of years by the time she was entered into therapy. That was considered a severe emotional disturbance, a covered disability.

The therapist decided that Mary's silence was a reaction to the stress she'd been through, and she needed to heal from the things that had happened to her. The therapist could see the child felt a real connection to this foster mother and she actually looked a lot like the foster mother.

Probably the foster mother looked a lot like her natural mother had looked and acted lovingly like her natural mother had acted. She connected beautifully with that woman.

To help Mary break the ice and start to communicate the therapist wrote a story for the little girl with the child seated beside her. She wrote a story about a little girl who had a terrible secret, and the secret was about something that had happened, and she couldn't even remember it very well except for some parts of it. It was so terrible, she couldn't talk about it. But it was so important she couldn't talk about anything else either because it wouldn't have been right to talk about anything else when she couldn't talk about this terrible thing that really needed to be talked about but was too terrible to talk about.

As the therapist told the story to the child, Mary just looked at the therapist silently with her huge eyes. Then the therapist took a little baby sock and put it on her hand, and drew a little face on the sock with no mouth. The therapist put the tiny sock on her fingers and showed it to the child. The therapist said, "This is what she feels like, with no mouth, just eyes and a nose,"
"She wishes she could talk, but she's not sure what to say."
"Maybe she'll talk to another little sock."
And the little girl's eyes looked surprised and interested.

So the therapist put another little hand drawn sock puppet on her other hand. This one had a mouth, and this one talked to the silent sock puppet.

124

After a while the therapist drew a mouth on the first little sock pocket and handed both socks to the child to take home. Within a week her foster mother reported that the child was talking again.

Additional social or a behavioral diagnosis would be in which a person frequently demonstrated behaviors that were not acceptable in public settings. For example, someone with a diagnosis of Tourette's might shout out highly charged words or a person with anxiety or obsessive compulsive disorder might not sit in their chair but continue to jump around the classroom, hopping around on one foot disrupting the classroom. These are behaviors in which pro-social skills are lacking. It could be a student who constantly grabs things from other students; or hits them and then runs away laughing; or someone who calls names or trips others just to see them fall.

At times this type of student can injure another, so they must be closely monitored, but in a kindly fashion. It is best when the teacher can show the child that their interest stems from wishing the child well, not from a perspective that they are just waiting to catch the child being bad. When most students see someone fall down the stairs they empathize, they recognize that the person could be injured. However, a child in this category has been known to push another student down the stairs because they thought it would look funny when the person fell, waving their arms and legs and screaming and going backwards down the staircase.

The child with a severe emotional disturbance may not realize the other person is 'like them' and feels pain and fear. Some children with SED seem to lack respect for others. Sometimes students in this category will break windows because they want to hear the glass break. They do not think of anyone else as having the same feelings they have and they don't connect with the humanness of others at times. Sometimes children in this category can be helped by learning to care for classroom pets. Such positive experiences may help them so that they will not torture or kill animals or smaller children who are weaker and more vulnerable than they are.

Many teachers report that students in this category are the least welcome in the class because they demonstrate behavior that disturbs the class and disturbs other students' learning. This is the area for which there is the least acceptance. These students are often given a diagnosis called severe emotional disturbance, and these are the who are most likely to have to attend school in a "self contained" classroom. They are also the students most likely to be sent to an institution (if they live in a state where there still are public institutions) because people find this kind behavior very disturbing and threatening, and it can be hurtful to others.

A severe emotional disturbance is a very hard thing to live with for the person who has it and for those who love that person. This is the group that generally speaking has the most trouble in their progress through school and their connection in any social setting. They are pushed out of every group they try to get into. They're not allowed in Boy Scouts, or

126

they're not allowed in the church choir, and when the case manager or their parent tries to connect them with others, people may give it a try, but when something happens they say the child "blew it." Generally speaking, it appears that students in this category tend not to connect at a meaningful level with adults, but the other children usually accept children with LD, if the parents have not cautioned them not to. It can take an enormous amount of work on the part of adults to connect with them.

It has been shown that people who have a severe emotional disturbance who experienced a traumatic event can often be helped, but often people who just develop these emotional disturbances on their own may not respond to therapy as readily.

Interestingly, teachers and staff are often angry at these students who push others, and who grab and break things for their bad behavior even though the student has a psychiatric diagnosis and a recognized disability. It is very difficult for some people to accept that a person might not have control over their behavior, it seems to go against reason. Therefore the student is reported or "written up" for "misbehaving". Many people don't seem to have an awareness of the enormous difficulty faced by a child who is driven to do things that are not acceptable to peers and to authority figures, and yet who is compelled and driven to do these behaviors anyway. It would be the most helpful to the student if authority figures were able to remain calm and unruffled. People should try to separate the action from the person, whenever they can.

Table 7: Social / Emotional Disturbance

Category II: Severe Emotional Disturbance
Typical Challenges for this group   • Off -task a lot of the time   • Can not work independently   • Has poor social skills
Best Practices for Classroom Instruction   • Keep the group small   • Provide constant supervision   • Teach cooperation by showing cooperation   • Give clear guidelines   • Don't change the rules as you go along   • Keep punishment to a bare minimum   • Never humiliate or embarrass student in hopes of gaining cooperation from him or her

Category 3: General Cognitive Delay

Amie

   Amie was given a low Apgar score at birth. She seemed to sleep a great deal more than most babies and was delayed in reaching milestones such as sitting, talking and walking. Amie likes to go to school. She enjoys coloring and art projects, but

she is bothered by getting her fingers sticky. She is interested
in the other children but they reject her, saying she is 'dumb
and clumsy'. She often does act in ways that the others
consider "too young for their age", doing things like picking
her nose or crying easily, and she is often confused about what
is going on or what is being talked about in the group. She
operates at a slower pace and enjoys tasks that take place with
one other person rather than in a large group.

General delay differs from learning disability in that students
with a learning disability have intelligence in the average or above range,
while students with a general cognitive slowness in every area. These are
students who learn more slowly, do not have relative strength in specific
academic areas but learn slowly across disciplines, and those whom it is
anticipated will continue to learn slowly throughout their academic
career. Many times students with this presentation are given a diagnosis
of mental retardation along one of the levels of the continuum on mental
retardation such as "borderline" or "mild", "moderate", or "severe".

Many students with a diagnosis of mental retardation may actually
have focal areas of the brain which lack enervation, and these students
may learn surprising better than expected once they "learn how to learn"
in their own unique way. Others continue to learn more slowly, perhaps
than their peers, but they achieve all of the necessary skills over time such
as reading, math and self-care. Many will go on to live busy and

129

productive lives in the community despite their early trouble in the academic setting.

Table 8: Mental Retardation

Category III: Mental Retardation
Typical Challenges for this group • Difficulty with complex tasks • Difficulty understanding relationships and making inferences. • Need for frequent rehearsal and review • Difficulty transferring information and skills to a new situation.
Best Practices for Classroom Instruction • Set realistic learning goals • Break work into small segments • Present information in a concrete format • Use hands-on learning • Use computer instruction where possible • Use real-life tasks where possible • Support student's peer relationships as a priority

Category 4: Physical or Sensory Disability

Glen: Sensory Disability

Glen is a popular junior in High School who has mastered the art of making everyone forget he is blind. He lost his sight at age 10 in an accident with a firecracker and has maintained his friendships with the same boys who were his constant companions in grade school.

When everyone else got their drivers license at age 16 some of the boys let him drive their dad's cars on a wide road, late at night. Glen uses computer accommodations in class, and has an aide assigned to read specific things aloud as needed. But he gets along pretty well overall, through his academic career.

At home his parents have helped him arrange his closet so that he can manage his morning routine and dress in clothing like that of his peers, and he takes part in all of the activities of his age group (movies, watching sports, and playing music). He plans to go to college with the gang, and become a computer programmer. He would like to serve in the Army in communications.

Mike: Physical Disability

Mike was in a car accident at age 12, and now uses a wheelchair for mobility. In grade school he was never seen without some type of sports equipment in his grip and he is secretly furious at his inability to take part in football and skateboarding with his old friends as he used to.

131

He is learning to ski (snow and water) and he plays on a wheelchair basketball league. Mike has also developed an interest in performing music and he is learning to play drums and guitar. He has written a few songs and thinks he'd like to be a musician when he grows up.

Mike is very sensitive to "being over helped" and resents it when people think they need to help him if he has not asked for help first. Mikes old friends often act like they don't see him in the hallway, but when they come face to face they are always friendly, if a bit distant. Mike is not sure where he fits, anymore. He see's himself as "disabled" and he is not comfortable with himself and his place in society.

Category four, physical and sensory disabilities, is related to mobility disabilities or students who are deaf or blind. Sensory disabilities can be acquired or present from birth as well. Sensory disabilities are anything, hearing, vision, smell, touch, or taste. These disabilities can be acquired, or they can be present from birth.

In physical and sensory disabilities, both inexperience and overprotection arise as characteristics that impact learning. Parents and teachers both tend to overprotect. One girl came to class riding in a wheelchair pushed by her aid,; and the aid said, "She can't do anything." That is overprotection. The aid meant to save the child from the embarrassment or the stress of trying to perform given the immense difficulties that she was facing around performance issues. But actually

132

that created a situation of inexperience for the child, and it needed to be changed. She needed protection but not overprotection.

It is possible that in cases in which a child has a physical or sensory disability the classroom pace could be too fast for them to explore. If a person has a great deal of trouble moving their hands and arms, moving rapidly through things that have to be manipulated, it's going to really put them behind and make it extremely difficult for them. Again it is just a matter of making an accommodation in the classroom.

Many people report that physical disabilities are the easiest for schools to accommodate, because the students seem to be getting along as well as to be expected. In some categories the complaint made is that no matter what the staff does to help, it doesn't work. In a physical disability it seems to staff that the time and money spent on the student has a visible and fairly rapid return on investment. Many also find that this category is the one in which most accommodations most readily occur during the school years. So perhaps it is not surprising that this group has the highest rate of graduation from high school. It has also been shown that this group finds it easiest to gain employment after graduate on from high school.

Table 9: Physical or Sensory Disability

Category IV: Mobility, Physical Disability
Typical Challenges for this group

- Average intelligence, or above
- May tire easily
- May have limited motor skill
- May find speech difficult

Best Practices for Classroom Instruction

- Try to keep learning goals the same as the rest of the class.
- Allow breaks when needed.
- Use computer instruction whenever possible
- Provide alternative ways to communicate
- Provide entrée to friendships during class time

Category 5: Advanced Cognitive Development

Dianne

Dianne surprised her mother when she was only 18 months old by fully dressing herself as she quietly listened in and followed the instructions mother was giving to Dianne's three-year old sister. When Mother turned around to dress Dianne, she was amazed to find Dianne already completely ready to go.

Dianne learned to read by silently following along in the books mother read out loud to her, and independently finding the words she learned from the children's book on other written material and on signs. When she was only two she wrote her first story, and in the story she described an awareness that she

134

would one day be older than her elder sister currently was. She learned all the words to songs on the radio, repeated poetry after she heard it once and could find any lost items in the house because she noticed where the adults put things, even when they were absent minded.

At home, Dianne read the encyclopedia and dictionary for fun. In school, Dianne had already read all of the library books in the elementary school library and all of the books in the children's section of the public library by the third grade, and was reading Freud on her own by fifth grade.

Category Five, then, is advanced cognitive development. These are the students who learn much more rapidly than the class as a whole, and they seek much more depth of learning. Students in this group constantly seek more information or they will become bored. They read the back of the chapter to find the references, they are the students who have read the whole book before the first day of class. They become very restless when the movement of the class stagnates or moves too slowly forward.

Advanced cognitive development is sometimes called "gifted and talented." Interestingly, students with learning disabilities are frequently also gifted. But the school is often quite unwilling to place a child in two categories, since they are unwilling enough to place students in even just in one are of special need. It complicates things. So the special and unique abilities of many children with learning disabilities are completely

135

missed because it's too expensive or just too much bother to have a child in both areas.

The fabulous thing about students with advanced cognitive ability is that they have a very large knowledge base. They remember easily what they've learned. They remember over time, and they have a greater depth of the knowledge and a greater depth of understanding to begin with. They make more interconnections between different categories of learning, and they're able to learn something in this setting and apply it in that one. There is a great deal of knowledge available, and they can manipulate and apply and use information to bring about synergy between diverse knowledge bases. Since they find their course work easy, they are often willing to help others in the classroom who find the assignment more challenging

Table 10: Advanced Cognitive Ability

Category V: Advanced Cognitive Ability
Typical Challenges for this group • Able to function at level of analysis and synthesis • Learn rapidly • Ability to think abstractly • Conceptual understanding of material, perhaps even before presented in class

- High ability to learn independently

Best Practices for Classroom Instruction

- Help student set challenging goals for independent learning
- Provide opportunity for students to pursue topics further on their own.
- Teach strategies for self instruction (library use, scientific method)
- Ask challenging questions to them
- Use advanced students as tutors if both they and the other student will benefit

Limitations of utilization of the charts

The goal of education is to maximize individual growth across all of those levels of students. When we talk about all students, we want all students to be in an optimal situation for learning and growth. As the people in charge, we are tasked with understanding what's known about how people learn. It's critical that a person teaching and that people who love and support students know what is possible for them. The sky is the limit. Someone once said, people are only limited by the imagination of those around them.

We need to learn how every particular student's developmental pattern is the same, and how it differs from a typical developmental pattern. Every child grows and develops with strengths in some areas and weaknesses in others. Some children are going to find it very easy to reach certain learning goals and very difficult to learn other learning goals. The chart above should be viewed as dynamic, meaning that the reader should remember that no student fits neatly in any of the student need categories. Every student has characteristics that are somewhat different from those typical in the center column. Therefore, for the good of each student, the possible learning and accommodation strategies need to be enlarged upon in a dynamic fashion, in a day-to-day fashion by everybody who has anything to do with this student.

The students each need to take the driver's seat in establishing what will work for them in their academic program. Students need to learn to analyze the situation, create a plan that they think might work, get some help in carrying it out, have a trial, do some evaluation and some further analysis. Then students should be supported in asking if their plan worked. The final step, mirroring that of the system process is for the student to lead a re-planning process through which they will identify and set another group of learning goals.

This needs to be done every week with every unit that the student is studying because this kind of math or geometry might be easier than that kind of math or algebra. It takes an enormous amount of energy to do this. As you recall from earlier in the semester, sometimes people grow

138

tired of working on the process of learning, especially if they can't get others on their team to join them. This is why people develop person-centered planning teams, because when one person is overwhelmed and discouraged, another can step to the front and provide the motivation and the encouragement that's needed to keep the team moving forward.

Additionally, everyone needs to have a circle of friends. A circle of friends is a very simple concept. It's just simply identifying people from the community that will be available to this child for many years. Some of the members of the circle should be peers, some could be relatives- both older relatives would bring wisdom and a historical knowledge of the family and of the world with them to the table, but who will depart before the child is elderly himself – and others siblings or cousins.

Chapter Two Thought Questions

After completing the reading of the chapter, read and write an essay to answer the following questions:

1. Contact the public school superintendent, the director of special education or a principal in your neighborhood public school. Ask them for a copy of the local school system's procedures and regulations for special education. This is a public document in the USA and is legally required to be available for all US citizens.

Review the documents given to you and report on the local regulations regarding Individual Educational Plans for children of school age with disabilities.

2. Imagine that you have been contacted by a family who has a child with special education needs. Go to one of the websites given to you in this Chapter (or another one) and report on an aspect of the website that you think that the family will find informative and helpful and explain what you will say when you share it with them, and how they can utilize the website to meet their needs.

3. Choose one of the categories of need for educational accommodation – such as Mental Retardation or Sensory Deficit or Learning Disability and describe what the classroom teacher can do to maximize the child's potential for educational success.

CHAPTER 3: Disability Epidemiology

Disability Numbers

In the previous chapter we covered some of the key points on how to work effectively and in a person centered way with someone who has a diagnosed disability. It may be of some help to gain an understanding of the numbers of people who have disabilities in the United States, and something about the types of disabilities diagnoses in the community. The 2000 U.S. Census6 shows us that 49.7 million people in the U. S. age 5 and over have a disability – that is nearly one person out of every five people living in the USA, or 19 percent of the total population.

About 5.2 million people with disability diagnoses were reported to be between the ages of 5 and 20 years. So, about 8% of people with disability diagnoses were in this school aged group.

At the time of the last census there were over 30.6 million people were between the ages of 21 and 64 years had been given disability diagnoses. A little over half (57%) of people in this group reported to the census takers that they were employed.

Some 14 million people with disability diagnose were aged 65 and over. Those with disabilities comprised 42% percent of people in this age group.

---

[6] U S 2006 Census http://www.census.gov/Press-Release/www/2002/demoprofiles.html

141

In Arkansas, Kentucky, Mississippi and West Virginia residents aged 5 and over had a disability in 2000 incidence of 24%, which was among the highest rates found in the nation.

At the other end of the spectrum, Alaska, Minnesota and Utah had disability rates around 15 percent, making these states among those with the lowest disability rates in the nation.

Across America the average percentage of people in a State with a disability diagnosis was about 19%. The range across States in the USA for disability diagnoses was 15% to 24%.

Earnings and Education

According to the March 2001 supplement to the Current Population Survey, the mean earnings in 2000 of year-round, full-time workers 16 to 64 with work disabilities was $33,109. By comparison, those workers of the same ages but without diagnosed disabilities earned an average of $43,269.

It has been reported that about 72% of people aged 16 years to 64 years, with a diagnosed disabilities had high school diplomas or some higher education in 2001.

Specifically, about 11% of people aged 16 to 64 with disabilities had college degrees or higher in 2001.

142

Specific Disabilities

According to a report titled "Americans With Disabilities: 1997," based on the Survey of Income and Program Participation, among people 15 and over in 1997:

- 25 million persons had difficulty walking a quarter mile or climbing a flight of 10 stairs, or used an ambulatory aid, such as a wheelchair (2.2 million) or a cane, crutches or a walker (6.4 million).

- About 18 million had difficulty lifting and carrying a 10-pound bag of groceries or grasping small objects.

- About 14.3 million had a mental disability, including 1.9 million with Alzheimer's disease, senility or dementia; and 3.5 million with learning disabilities.

- About 8.0 million had difficulty hearing what was being said in a normal conversation with another person (even when wearing a hearing aid); of these, 800,000 were unable to hear what was said in a normal conversation.

- About 7.7 million had difficulty seeing the words and letters in ordinary newspaper print (even with glasses); of these, 1.8 million were unable to see words and letters in ordinary newspaper print.

The preceding facts come from Census 2000, the Current Population Survey and the Survey of Income and Program Participation.

Societal Disability Models

The present service system is the result of a series of shifts in disability perspectives, known as disability models[7].

Although developmental disability, mental retardation or cognitive disability may be discussed and understood within several frameworks, for instance the moral model of disability, the educational model, or the minority model of disability, human services in the United States have been designed on the medical model of disability[8]. Let's review each of the more common models briefly before moving on to discuss the "gold standard" in disability models, the Strengths Model.

The Moral Model

The oldest model of disability describes a system of superstitious "placing of blame" for a disability on a deserved punishment of the person, or the person's parents or even the person's community. The disability is seen as a tragedy, and at times it has even been said that an infant born with a disability was being punished for misbehavior in a previous life. In the Moral Model of disability, simple malevolent evil spirits have been implicated in the bestowing of a disability, as well as more complex religious explanations involving everything from serving as a moral example to others, to serving as a way for others to raise their

---

[7] *Excerpted from Exploring Self Advocacy from a Social Power Perspective* (Whitehead & Hughey, 2004).

[8] Mackelprang & Salsgiver, 1999

moral status through offering assistance to the person with a disability diagnosis.

The Educational Model

The extensively pervasive model of expert intervention needed to "teach away" the disability has been termed the Educational Model. In this perspective in-depth evaluation of the person by a team of experts is followed by aggressive treatment plans used to "remediate" the person and cause them to "graduate" up a series of pre-set standards until the disability is "overcome".

The Minority Model

The model of disability as a social construct grants a civil rights perspective to disability so that people with disabilities are viewed as an underprivileged or protected social group such as that of race or gender. The minority model calls for people with disabilities to learn how they can band together as a group and demand legislation to protect their rights and to remove barriers from full civic participation.

The Medical Model

Viewed from the perspective of the medical model, a person is assessed against a standard of normalcy. The person is regarded to be deficient in some important way. The elements of the person found to fall outside the range of accepted normal limits are diagnosed as dysfunctional. Services are directed and controlled by professional experts, since it is believed that without expert management of services consumers would not know how to, or would not do, what was best for them. The "consumer" plays a passive role as a patient under this model. As in the educational model, plans are made to remediate the person so that the disability can be "overcome".

The Strengths Model

The most recent model of disability to have gained widespread acceptance is that which acknowledges the areas in which a person may need accommodation without ever losing sight of the person's unique talents, abilities, interests and strengths. Life planning from the strengths model centers around the person's interests, with the person in the "drivers seat" and acting as the lead person in the planning process.

Historically people with developmental disabilities and mental illness were housed with criminals or with indigent medical patients[9], which is still the case in prisons and some hospitals. In the 1830s Dorothea Dix worked to reform the American system of housing patients with mental illness among those in hospitals for physical illness. She proposed that quiet and well appointed homes (to be known as "asylums") should be built to offer people with mental illness and cognitive disabilities shelter from the stresses of life on the outside. It was thought at the time that anyone would prefer institutionalization to the difficulties of a life in the community.

_____

[9] Bradley & Knoll, 1990; Schwartz, 1992

146

After the first modern asylum was built in Worchester, Massachusetts in 1833, the model spread widely. By 1955, over 500,000 Americans lived in state mental institutions across the United States. Not only were adults identified and placed in institutions after failure in a generic social setting, but people began to be institutionalized at very young ages, often at birth. Many people spent their entire lives in an institution, despite never having demonstrated an inability to care for themselves or to participate successfully in society. Gradually, as the number of people receiving care in institutions increased, the original goal of system reform and protective care declined, and interactions between staff and patients became less flexible. Concurrently professional hierarchical treatment protocol, lead by professional experts, and thin staffing left little opportunity to address individual needs and preferences of the people the system was designed to serve.

Beginning the wave of reform in the 1970's, lawsuits on the behalf of institutionalized persons challenged the right of the state to forcibly institutionalize citizens who had broken no law. This was a time of rapid and complex changes in the system of services for people with developmental disabilities, as it was in society at large. It was, particularly, an era of shifting in widely held conceptions of physical disability. This dramatic change in public sentiment in the 1970's resulted in the release of approximately 75% of patients in state institutions.

The restructuring of the system from institution-based to community-based between 1977 and 1990 was characterized by movement of people from large facilities to small congregate care "residential service settings" commonly known as group homes. By 1990 the number of people in American institutions was vastly reduced. Current data shows that while some people using service system funds live in their own homes or with family members, many others continue to live in state run or private group home congregate care settings. These settings may be owned, rented or managed by residential services providers who provide care, supervision, instruction, and other support to consumers.

While most (forty-three) states continue to operate at least one large mental retardation/ developmental disability (MR/DD) facility in 2003, the number of people in residence continues to fall. In 1998 the ratio of institutionalized persons was 19 persons in the large state facilities per 100,000 of the general population, a substantial decline from the 1967 ratio of 99.7 persons per 100,000. The decrease is due to several factors. Since fewer parents have institutionalized their children at birth the number of children and youth in the large state MR/DD facilities continued to decrease rapidly, contributing to the aging of the institutionalized population.

However, community services for people with disabilities have not kept pace with deinstitutionalization. There are now a reported 100,000 persons on state waiting lists to receive residential services.

In recent years a new type of service delivery has developed. Services of many types, such as education and health care, are now being provided to people with developmental disabilities in integrated or generic settings by agencies that have traditionally provided services only to the generic population. Since people with disabilities are now being service by both disability and generic agencies, there is an increased need for consumers to learn to navigate both types of systems successfully.

With a shift in agency target populations that accommodates both people with disabilities and the generic population, decisions about services cannot be made without reference to the overall structure of agencies. Correspondingly, decisions about the operation of programs and services for the generic community can no longer be made without specific reference to the accommodation needs of the people with disabilities who will be integrated within the agency service population[10].

A Short History of Disability

Historically the public has appeared to be perplexed about the meaning of disability, and therefore it is not surprising that there has been confusion over how to best support people with disabilities.

Whether people with disabilities have been feared, revered, pitied or admired, they have always been stigmatized by a "labeled identity" that is

---

[10] National Council on Disability 2003

based solely upon their disability. People with a disability label have faced a deeply seated and widespread prejudice against disability[11]. Predominant societal attitudes have tended to keep people with disabilities isolated from the mainstream, and this denied them participation in the full range of civic, educational employment and religious activities. Such isolation, in turn, contributes to the maintenance of stereotypical attitudes toward people with disabilities[12] and impacts their own beliefs about what is possible for them.

People with disabilities are popularly believed to differ from other people in some important way.

As a group they are generally assumed to be weak, sick, or to have a progressive (and perhaps communicable) disease. Since people with disabilities are often thought of as sick, society expects them to fulfill the sick role, even when they are healthy. As sick people they are not expected to be productive, to contribute to society, nor to be independent or self-sufficient. Should a person need an attendant for physical assistance, the sick role is all but impossible to shake. Instead of being able to direct their own care, a consumer must depend upon doctors to write "orders" for even over-the-counter medicines[13]. They must rely on professionals to select their personal home health aides.

---

[11] Diller, 1998
[12] Mackelprang & Salsgiver, 1999
[13] Schwartz, 1992

150

Since staff who support people with disabilities often believe that they work for an agency rather than for the person with disability whom they serve[14], as mentioned earlier, professional employees of the system retain positions of higher status or professional worth than the people for whom they work, as well as occupying positions of greater control.

Most observers could list many ways in which paid staff routinely exercise a higher than necessary level of control over those who rely on them for services. This approach to *helping* almost certainly reflects underlying assumptions of both staff and the general public about disability[15], and is supported, even demanded by the culture of service agencies.

At times individuals with disabilities are seen to rise above the expected limitations of the disability and serve as an inspiration[16] (the old Moral Model in action). But in general people with disability diagnoses are presumed to be non-productive, dependent, and consumers of system care "packages" (as shown in the Educational and Medical Models described above). The mistaken perception that people with disabilities are a menace to society[17] has been well documented, and is illustrated by the way that societal fears led to the original policy of forced

---

[14] Mackelprang & Salsgiver, 1999
[15] Schwartz, 1992
[16] Diller, 1998
[17] Rhodes, 1993; Mackelprang & Salsgiver, 1999

institutionalization, segregation, marriage restrictions, and the widespread sterilization of people with disabilities.

Sometimes people with disabilities are believed to be a menace to society either due to a supposed inherent evil nature or simply by virtue of the danger that they might reproduce and burden society with "more disabled people[18]." Because these attitudes are reflected in public policies that address disability, these ambivalent attitudes need to be clearly understood by people with disabilities and their guardians who want to effectively negotiate with the service system.

People without disabilities have often tended to devalue and stigmatize people with disabilities in ways that are analogous to the treatment of other minority groups (here is the Minority Model in action). However, many people with a disability have rejected the assumption that their disability makes them so very different from others. They have struggled to redefine disability as the product of a disabling society, rather than a problem created by real limitation or loss[19].

According to Campbell and Oliver in Disability Politics, to acquire a disability-- or to come out of the closet with a hidden disability-- is to experience "the entire collapse of one's social standing."

---

[18] Nagler, 1990
[19] Campbell & Oliver, 1996

152

Despite these realities isolation is not inevitable, it is due to the social meaning that others place on the disability- or the "social construct" of disability. When a person is given the professional label "disabled" they are frequently also labeled "deviant" as well and assigned a societal position with role expectations based upon stereotypes and myths about disability – "persons with disabilities are dangerous, sick, or incompetent." Even today, beyond a vague expectation that people with disabilities will be looked after by professional staff, most people without disability know little about disability or the day to day living conditions of people with disabilities. It is the thesis of this book that the isolation and degraded life options imposed upon many people with disabilities is the result of often hidden and virtually unexplored dynamics of social power.

Although this is rapidly changing, in most of America due to an antiquated system structure established under a medical model of disability, the human service system continues to force people to trade their basic freedoms for professionally-directed services and supports[20].

Over 7 million individuals with disabilities rely on medical and supportive services covered by Medicaid[21]. However, if working-age individuals with disabilities increase their self-sufficiency through employment, they jeopardize the only health insurance available to

---

[20] Pence, 1995
[21] GAO 03-587

them[22] since benefits are usually revoked once a person is employed. An "either – or" situation is created for people with a disability by system constraints. They must first obtain the status "Disabled" in order to access employment, health insurance and support services. Among the proffered services is employability training. However the designation "Disabled" is given only if the person proves that they are *unable to work*. If, after receiving the designation of "Disabled", people undertake available employment training, prepare for and find gainful employment- then they lose entitlement to insurance coverage and other services, since they are no longer be "unable to work"- a requirement of the designation "Disabled". Again, in order to access to employability training services the person must demonstrate that they are unemployable. If they become partially employable after the training, they are taken off the entitlement list. Given that the average earned income of people in this group is less than $800 per month[34] the loss of insurance and an SSI stipend is too high a cost to pay for employment.

Alternately, a person might forgo the designation of "Disabled" but they would then be barred from receiving the services that could lead to self-sufficiency. Further, in regard to accessibility, availability, affordability and adequacy of services, entitlement programs have been enacted *without fiscal entitlement*. People may well meet the eligibility

---

[22] GAO 03-587

154

criteria of a program and still be denied services since funding for the program is discretionary[23].

In the disability community it is known that prominent among the barriers to lives in the community are disincentives to work caused by inconsistent national policies based upon antiquated models of both disability and realistic employment opportunity.

Despite receiving services from arguably the most costly system of care in the world, people receiving services most often live in poverty[24]. In recent years there has been a Federal U.S. MR/DD budget of some 25 billion dollars annually, but the people for whom the system exists have very little control over how resources are spent to support them. As designated by Congress they have a per capita dollar amount of over $90,000 per person, but they completely lack the right to spend it in ways of their own choosing. The funds filter through so many levels of government and staff that little money reaches the person directly. In isolation from the generic community, people who use system dollars are trapped for the most part in congregate care in homes they did not choose, with roommates they did not select, served by staff they did not hire and cannot fire.

---

[23] National Council on Disability 2003
[24] Schwartz, 1992; Nerney, 1998; Callahan & Mank, 1998; Prouty & Larkin, 1999

Chapter Three Thought Questions

After completing the reading of the chapter, write an essay answering the following questions:

1. What has the history of services for people with disabilities been in this country?

2. What are some of the social and political barriers faced by people with disabilities in this country?

3. What are your ideas about what might help to overcome some of the barriers against full participation that people with disabilities face today?

CHAPTER 4 : Finding Resources

After reading the material in Chapters 1 through Chapter 3, you should begin to have a sense of the most helpful ways a person can approach disability services and supports in education and employment areas.

In order to move to the next stage of knowledge, a person must step actively into the process of finding "what is out there" and becoming adept at managing the various healthcare and intervention services that have been created for persons with disabilities by foundations, institutions, nonprofit agencies and the government. In today's world, we start with the internet.

To keep track of your new-found knowledge, create a three ring binder with information from the following organizations and government agencies, as well as any others you are able to find through a search of the internet, a discussion with someone you know, and a look through the local phone book. Print the home page and other helpful information from each site, or type a summary of services on a fresh sheet, and place all of the information in a three-ring binder for ready reference.

157

General Reference:

Disabilityinfo.gov is a comprehensive federal website of disability-related government resources.

School District :

The position of the federal government, with the No Child Left Behind Act is: *"Education is a key determinant of future success, and every American deserves equal access to education."*

EXPLORE YOUR LOCAL SERVICES

http://www.disabilityinfo.gov/digov-
public/public/FindSL.do?categoryId=61

NICHCY has a wealth of information on disabilities!

NICHCY stands for the *National Dissemination Center for Children with Disabilities.* We serve the nation as a central source of information on:

- disabilities in infants, toddlers, children, and youth,
- IDEA, which is the law authorizing special education,
- No Child Left Behind (as it relates to children with disabilities), and
- research-based information on effective educational practices.

http://www.nichcy.org/

State Department of Health:

Health care is a central issue for people with disabilities. Finding affordable health care and obtaining adequate health care coverage have been among the greatest obstacles to independent living, employment and full participation in their communities. The federal government recognizes that people with disabilities should not be hindered in acquiring health care or health insurance. The importance of quality health care goes far beyond physical conditions. Mental health issues are now given the prominence and coverage they deserve.

CENTER FOR DISEASE CONTROL (CDC)
   http://www.cdc.gov/ncbddd/dh/default.htm

FIRE SAFETY FOR PEOPLE WITH DISABILITIES
   http://www.usfa.dhs.gov/citizens/disability/

HEALTH RESOURCE AND SERVICES ADMINISTRATION (US GOV)
   Health Centers provide health and dental care to people of all ages, whether or not they have health insurance or the money to pay for health care. http://www.hrsa.gov/help/

STATE BY STATE MENTAL HEALTH SERVICES INFORMATION

http://mentalhealth.samhsa.gov/databases/

Professional Organizations

NCWD/Youth is your source for information about employment and youth with disabilities. Our partners — experts in disability, education, employment, and workforce development — strive to ensure you will be provided with the highest quality, most relevant information available. http://www.ncwd-youth.info/

INFORMATION FOR SERVICE WORKERS

http://www.dswresourcecenter.org/index.php/dsw

The National Direct Service Workforce (DSW) Resource Center supports efforts to improve recruitment and retention of direct service workers who help people with disabilities and older adults to live independently and with dignity.

This Resource Center provides state Medicaid agencies, researchers, policymakers, employers, consumers, direct service professionals, and other state-level government agencies and organizations easy access to information and resources they may need about the direct service workforce.

Training

DO IT! http://www.washington.edu/doit/

DO-IT serves to increase the participation of individuals with disabilities in challenging academic programs and careers. It promotes the use of computer and networking technologies to increase independence, productivity, and participation in education and employment.

The National Association for Adults with Special Learning Needs' goal is to ensure that adults with special learning needs have the opportunities necessary to become successful lifelong learners. www.naasln.org

Parent Support

ANSWERS FOR FAMILIES: http://www.answers4families.org/assisted/
USA Federal Site www.disabilityinfo.gov

Accommodation Information for work http://www.ada.gov/
Toll-Free ADA Information Line
Call to obtain answers to general and technical questions about the ADA and to order technical assistance materials:
800-514-0301 (voice) 800-514-0383 (TDD)

CHAPTER 5: Supporting Others in Moving From School To Career

Introduction To Moving From School to Career

The Special Education Law requires that transition planning to help a student move from school to a career must start at the age of 14 for a person with an Individual Educational Plan, an IEP. However, planning for transition from school to a career should really start when the child is about the age of 3 years.

Thinking back through your own childhood, you probably can remember people asking you the question, "What do you want to be when you grow up?" when you were in preschool. You probably said, "A Nurse, A Doctor, A Fire Fighter, A Police Officer" or some other work with which you were familiar. Even though your early identification with a future work role probably did not stay the same through the intervening years, the question created your awareness that you would grow up, and that when you grew up you would be expected to contribute to society by working.

Clearly, then, all children need to be approached with questions about their preferred line of work from early ages, so that the self image all children hold is of themselves as a valued worker who contributes to society. You would probably be amazed to learn that some adults have never been asked the question, "What do you want to be when you grow up?" Many children with disabilities are not encouraged to dream of their future as a successful adult.

It is not only persons with disabilities who need some level of a "hand up" when they are moving from school into the workforce. Everyone needs help in moving from childhood to adulthood, from school to a career. A wide variety of people can be of some help in the process. Classroom teachers, parents, adult friends, and job coaches all play a role in preparing children to think about the roles they would like to play when they are grown. Those of us who value inclusion also need to learn how to support employers, so that employers learn value the contribution that people with special needs can make to their work settings.

The commitment we make to personally taking part in the effort to generate community commitment to school-to-career training is necessary because work settings have been segregated for many years, and many employers do not see it as being their role to accommodate everyone. The community is just so large that many employers think they can simply find a new employee who does not need training or accommodation. Those who want to employ people with disabilities often fear that the cost of accommodations will be too high, or they are fearful of doing something the wrong way. So, people who value inclusion have to be the ones who get the word "inclusion" out into the community, so they can generate commitment to inclusion throughout the general community.

In its simplest form, school-to-career is a way to make learning relevant to a person's life. If learning occurs only in the classroom but real life occurs everywhere else, the learning in the classroom becomes stilted and stagnated, and it is less connected to the rest of the person's life. School-to-career brings the classroom out into the community and brings the community into the classroom. Also in school-to-career experiences people (both employers and students) learn how to build an effective community network of opportunity for people with special needs.

You may recall from Chapter 1 the story about the young man who wanted to be a model and how a way had to be found so that his dream could became his reality. The story about the young man who wanted to play football is also a good example of a community network being created by asking the question, "*who do you know that's involved in football and how can we start a conversation around opportunity for a person with special needs who loves football?*"

School-to-career has also helped in educational planning. A person who graduates from high school and then goes to college without any connection to the working world is at a disadvantage when it comes time for them to choose a major in college. If they have not had community experiences, they don't know enough about the community to figure out where they might best fit in. Similarly, a person who graduates from high school and enters the workforce would have little idea of how to start a career, if school-to-career had not been a component of their education all along the way. A person entering vocational training straight from high school has little idea which way to turn. If the first time a person considers a career, they are at a serious disadvantage.

So school-to-career should be a component of education for every person. But as we learned from Chapter 1 in our person-centered planning discussion, people from vulnerable populations not only have even a deeper need and a more immediate need for school-to-career services and school-to-career discussions to be in place around their education, *they are often the very group excluded from that opportunity.*

All students need school-to-career opportunities. (All means <u>all</u>!)

Many teachers have been in the classroom literally all of their lives. They entered preschool at age three years, and completed college at age 23 years at which time they entered the classroom as a teacher. All educators need to be connected with people in the world outside of their classroom, because the world outside is the world in which their students will be working. Educators need to keep abreast of changes in the needs of employers, so they can prepare their students. Teachers and educators need to be connected with the outside world through summer activities in the field in which they teach. For example, a math teacher could benefit from a summer internship in a math application field in research or nonprofit accounting, or the space program. Wherever the interest of the educator lies, they can seek and serve a summer internship. The very process of exploring the outside world for their internship opportunity, applying and serving it will enhance their performance in the classroom. It will bring a deep connection to real life into the material they present and the way that they view their student's futures.

In the same way that educators need to be connected to the working world outside of the classroom, business people need to be connected with schools. If education happens in a vacuum and business happens in a vacuum, future workers will find it difficult to be successful in preparing to work and businesses will have to provide extensive training for new employees.

People in education and people in business need to stay in touch with the work each other are doing all the way along, so that students can hit the ground running when they enter their working lives. Everyone in the community plays a role in the process of preparing young people for careers. People are educators, business people, or students. Those people who simultaneously serve in two of the three roles are well prepared to help students move into the workforce successfully. A full community-wide effort is necessary to ensure that school-to-career is a meaningful part of education for everyone.

Labor Force Profile

At present, twenty-nine percent of adults with disabilities (29%) are employed. Disappointingly the research shows that over seventy percent (70%) of people with disabilities (PWD) want to be employed but they don't have the opportunity.

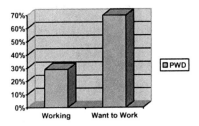

Figure 3: Disparity Between PWD Working Vs. Those Who Want To Work

The record reports a smaller percentage of people as "wanting to work" than is really the case, because many of the people who want to work have given up and they are no longer looking for work.

It has been said that the federal government spends more than forty times as much money to support nonworking people with disabilities than it would cost to prepare them for work. Perhaps this is one reason the government established the Americans with Disabilities Act to help people get jobs. However, working is out of the reach of many people with disabilities, and many member of the potential workforce are relying on SSI disability insurance or Social Security to survive.

About a quarter of people with disabilities (25%) did not have the opportunity to graduate from high school compared to nine percent (9%) in the general population.

Well-meaning people wonder how that happens in the land of opportunity. Here is one example of the process as it could unfold.

John's Story

John was identified as being a student with special needs in Kindergarten and he was given an individual educational plan. He entered first grade with a cohort of fifty students. Eighteen of these students were held back and repeated first grade a second time. After the second time through the First  Grade, all of the students in the cohort, whether failing each year or not, were passed through each subsequent grade until they reached high school. Each had an Individual Education Plan (IEP) that was reviewed once per year.

In high school all eighteen of the students in the cohort were segregated into the lowest levels of courses offered, and most were funneled into vocational coursework.

Only one student of the original cohort of eighteen students graduated at the same time as his peers who did not have IEPs twelve years earlier, in Kindergarten. Only one student with an IEP was able to complete enough credits in the correct coursework to graduate when the students without IEPs graduated from high school. His comment at the time was that he made it through to graduation *in spite of the school's effort*, rather than because of it.

The following year when the second set of the original eighteen students in the cohort should have graduated a year later than their peers, two more students with IEPs had completed enough credit hours to graduate.

By the next year (when the students were aged 20 years) each of the remaining fifteen students with IEPs had dropped out of school. Students with disabilities are entitled to stay in high school until the age of 21, but they did not see a purpose in it since they knew they could never accumulate enough credits to graduate.

Persistence to Graduation

By following the cohort of eighteen children who had IEPs in Kindergarten through high school in an otherwise high-performing school district, and finding that only three of them were able to graduate from high school, we have revealed a significant delay in graduation rates of students with IEPs. In this case the seventeen of the eighteen students in the cohort were delayed from high school by two to three years; and most (83%) never earned a high school diploma. In fact, most of the people with disabilities (PWD) dropped out of school one or two years earlier than they were entitled to be educated. It is unfortunate that this story is not unique to one school district. It is common.

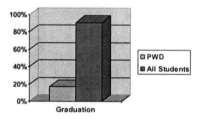

Figure 4: Graduation Rates of PWD vs. Others.

Finding Work Without A High School Diploma

It is very difficult to find employment without a high school degree.

If people with disabilities had jobs so that they could support themselves, it would save the government billions of dollars. The record shows that it would save $1.8 billion in Social Security, and $286 million in food stamps. Assuring that people with disabilities could earn a high school degree could remove 284,000 people from Medicaid and 166,000 people from Medicare. But the most important difference it would make if people with disabilities worked in the community would be that these citizens would be able to become true community members. They would shop and buy goods and services. They would own their own homes.

They would be save for their own futures. They would be contributing members of society, which is just what they want to be.

Table 11: Benefits of Employment

BENEFITS OF EMPLOYMENT FOR PEOPLE WITH DISABILITIES
Government Savings: $1,800,000 Social Security $2,860,000 Food Stamps
Social Benefits: People would be full members of the community. People would buy goods and services. People would buy their own homes. People would save for their futures.

Barriers To Employment

But the barriers placed in their way have kept being self supporting from becoming a reality for them.

Statistically, the recorded employment rate is lowest among people who need an attendant. That is, if a person has a special need that requires them to have an attendant, they are less likely to be able to finish high school with a high school diploma, and they are less able or less likely to enter the workforce as an employee.

The employment rate is said to be the highest among those people who report a sensory disability or those who use a wheelchair. Statistically, the least likely person to be employed is someone with multiple disabilities. For every person who is unemployed and looking, there is another person who has given up looking for work, but would take a job if one were offered.

At one time special education did not exist. People with special needs were simply not allowed in the educational system. Then, special education was established, but it was seen more as a root to an alternative life outside the mainstream flow, or a route to a special sector of life in a religious or institutional setting, not as a way to prepare for a real life in the community. Now that specter has changed, but the *person* who is at the center of the plan is still most often overlooked.

The Evolution Of Special Education

Special Education has come a long way, but there is still need for improvement in most settings.

Special education is often seen as a comprehensive approach to a program development that aligns student goals with educational experiences and with services and supports. We are no longer talk about a specific track on which students with disabilities are automatically placed. In previous times, students with special needs were herded onto a special education track that would chug along like a train towards a uniform goal for a segregated life. Now people with disabilities are accorded individual civil rights for an Individual Education Plan. The next step for education to collectively take is to learn how to prepare an Individual Educational Planning *process* that always delivers an planning for individuals in which their personal dreams, hopes, needs and preferences at the very core of the planning process. This will be person centered planning, in a nutshell.

What is needed is a widespread practice of implementing school-to-career planning and activities for students with special needs or students with disabilities that prepare them for working lives in the community. Part of the person-centered planning needs to be focused around the student's own role in the planning process, so student-focused planning is the critical first step. There needs to be a very high level of family involvement as well as cooperation between agencies and disciplines of professionals, as well, for this process to be effective.

School-to-career components predict postsecondary success for all students. Every student needs to start with career awareness training and the process should start at the age of preschool with an exploration of careers. All children need to be told that they are expected to work when they are grown and every child should be exposed to a wide range of careers that children of their age are developmentally able to find interesting. This level of career exploration is known as career awareness.

Research has shown that having two or more job experiences within the final two years of high school is strongly correlated with success after high school graduation (Whitehead, 2001[25]). In this study success was defined as "a person having full-time employment; or part-time employment and part-time education enrollment; or full-time educational enrollment". Lack of "success" was defined as a person sitting at home doing nothing; which is what happened to most of the people with special needs who did not graduate from high school.

Preparing For A Career

In order to make success a reality for everyone, job strategy training must be put in place. People don't naturally just know how to go about getting a job, how to identify an interest, how to train and prepare for that interest educationally and how to get practical experience and learn job success skills. Job strategy training is a critical component of success.

Built into the ADA legislation is a component that entitled people with special needs and people with disabilities the right to reasonable accommodations in the workplace so that they can be employed in the community. This civil right parallels the rights granted by the IDEA Act which entitled children to attend free and appropriate educational settings in their community (that is, that they can attend regular classrooms in the local public schools), and which also now requires transitional planning from school to career for all students aged 14 and older.

---

[25] Whitehead (2001) Learning Exchange Study on School to Career

ACTION STEP:

Go online and find the ADA website from the government home
site of www.firstgov.gov

One reason that the law is not fully implemented in each setting is that
school-to-career transition is often regarded by busy teachers as another
add-on; something else that they have to do that no one funds, rewards or
evaluates.

While people mean well, most often, they have a great deal of work to
do and the responsibility to create school-to-career opportunities often
slips through the cracks because it is not well monitored.

Part of the problem is that the business community and educational
systems have historically been separate. Sometimes people in either area
might be territorial and want to protect themselves, their positions, or
their employees. This could make them less sensitive to the needs of the
community at large. What can be done to bring the two systems into
closer collaboration?

Coordinated technical assistance is one way that people with special
needs will be able to prepare for and enter the work force. Assistive
technology created for school-to-career that belongs to individuals and
transfers from home to school to work must become a component of the

daily life of children with special needs throughout their educational years, it can not be "added on" afterward.

School To Career Planning

School-to-career planning needs to include all students; including those with special needs of every kind, students with disabilities, students from migrant working families, students from disadvantaged circumstances of every kind, especially economic, and historically underserved populations. The business community, educators, parents and students all need to be included from the ground up in the comprehensive planning process. If the process were to be designed only for students with disabilities, the processes will never happen across educational settings in a systematic manner and implementation would become an "add-on" for teachers who are already busy.

The process then needs to become personal for each student. Someone must identify what the barriers are between each student and a successful outcome in the working world, and then help the student and their family build a bridge to close the gaps. There needs to be teamwork between special education and regular education teachers. There needs to be teamwork between schools as students move upward in the system. Many students with special need to attend more than one school simultaneously. For example, they start the day in their local school, at midday take a bus to a special education school or a vocational training school, and then return to their school of origin to attend afternoon classes before taking the bus home.

There also needs to be teamwork between schools and businesses. People in the business community need to come into the schools and serve as mentors. People in the working community need to come into the schools and give workshops and presentations so that students are aware of what is available to them in the community and what opportunities they have in the community. Knowing about how classroom learning is utilized in work settings makes learning more relevant. If a child is having trouble learning math, and they don't see any practical application for math in any time in their future, then they are not motivated to try. Once they realize that they want to learn math to help them enter an exciting job in the workforce, they will work harder at learning. Learning becomes relevant.

We also need to get students out of the school and into the community through Job Shadows and Internship programs starting in about the seventh grade, so that they can begin to envision themselves as successful adults, working for a living.

Preparation Timeline For School to A Career

Table 12: School to Career Stages

PreSchool, Kindergarten-Grade 3 Career Awareness
Grade 4 – 6 Career Exploration
Grade 7 -12 Job Shadows and Internships
Grade 11 – 12 Two jobs in the community

As shown above, school-to-career planning starts in pre-kindergarten with three year olds who need to learn awareness. They need to learn that they are expected to be self-supporting in their future and they need to learn about the kinds of jobs available in their community. While a three-year-old may not maintain lifelong interest in the same type of career they find exciting at a young age, their main need is to be aware that they will be working adults one day.

Career Exploration for grade-schoolers covers the wide array of different jobs a person might learn to do. Grade school aged children need to understand the ways in which their classroom education will teach them the essential skills that it takes to carry out various jobs. They need to see the connection between their spelling list and work; their

179

math assignments and work; and the role science and social studies will play in their future knowledge base.

By Junior High or Middle School there needs to be an opportunity for true exploration of jobs in the community. Students of this age need to leave the classroom and enter individual job settings through Job Shadows, internships, and "practica" opportunities. Making a connection with the real world is a strong motivator for them to do well in difficult, challenging academic work because the student sees the relevance in learning that challenging material in their future life.

Career planning must start at the age of three or four years for all children; and if the student has special needs, it is especially important that they are at the center of the planning process and that their talents, their abilities, their strengths and their interests are at the very center of the planning process. This model of disability perspective is, as you know, called the *Strengths Model.*

In one survey, students with disabilities were asked how schools could increase the level of knowledge and understanding among young people with disabilities so that hey can remove their own barriers.

They said, "We need to learn self-determination skills."

Many students with disabilities felt that they had spent many years being told what they should do and how they should do it. They reported that they had been subjected to behavior modification and "rewarded and punished" for so many years that they had lost a sense of self-determination. They had little sense of who they were, what their talents might be, and what it was they wanted out of their lives.

Students with disabilities have asked for training in self-determination to connect them with their own goals and their own ability to make discriminatory plans for their own lives.

Students also wanted empowerment to move forward on their self-set goals. The students with disabilities said, "We come up with things we want sometimes, but then we don't have any way to carry it out."

What is meant by the term *self-determination*? Self -determination is the ability to control your own life and to achieve your own self-defined goals. While self-determination is essential to freedom, it is dependent upon access to information.

Training in self-determination must start in early childhood and it can only develop in an environment of social support. People who know what they want and who try to meet their own goals are called "self-determined" in settings where authority figures value person centered planning. However, if there is no social support for self-determination and a person is assertive about meeting their needs, they are branded "a troublemaker".

As the barriers against people with disabilities become clearer to them, many people wonder what they can do to help. There is always a way to reach out and help someone else. If you are already connected with students in school- as a parent or an advocate or as a teacher- you can build self-confident learners. Regardless of what a person's special needs might be or what the barriers to learning are, people can become self-confident learners if they are not criticized, if they are not embarrassed, if they are not told constantly what they can't do and how far behind others they are. Their diagnosis should never be publically stated or used as a reason to explain their performance.

A self-confident learner: sets their own pace, learns how to set their own goals and learns how to reward themselves for reaching their own goals.

That process, itself, is what builds self-confidence. Here, again, we are really talking about individualizing instruction. Instruction need not be "one size fits all" but instead should be based upon individually established goals and individually established outcomes, and individually established timelines. Educational plans need to depend upon the self-motivation of the student to participate. That is the first priority in education.

If you are in an employment setting the way to help is to make it known that you will assist in getting accommodations in place for a worker, a job shadow or an intern. People need mentors. They need job shadows and internships to be open to them so that there is an entrée to the working world. Connections need to be routinely developed between school and work in the community.

In a living environment you can help by assuring that you consistently ask the people you support for their preferences, and then you must respond by carrying out the task in the way they asked you to. This builds self-confidence in the person, too.

We did a survey a couple of years ago through the Learning Exchange[26] in the Business / Education partnership to find out what Kansas City employers thought were the most important of all of the skills and abilities that a new worker might enter the field having in their portfolio.

In response to the question 85% of employers said that "the person needs to have the capability to work cooperatively with others".

The second most common response at 83% of employers was that "employees must understand appropriate workplace appearances".

---

[26] Greater Kansas City, Missouri and Kansas

Following these responses were: "trustworthiness", "good communication skills", and "appropriate behavior in dealing with clients".

Among the 450 employers in metropolitan greater Kansas City who responded to this survey, the responses did not address actual workplace skills (such as typing or knowledge) until after the issues related to social skills had been listed. Educators and families need to be aware that social skills were the primary need of employers, so that students will be trained in social skills. Students must be able to graduate and enter workplace settings prepared to succeed.

Need for Accommodations

We always speak about people with disabilities needing accommodations as if it is an unusual situation. In fact, that every student needs accommodations of one type or another. As teachers, staff, employers and community members we accommodate all students on behalf of their age, their developmental level, their level of inexperience, and their vocabulary. We do it without even thinking about it, unless the youngster has a visible disability.

When we are talk about accommodating students with special needs, we should acknowledge the fact that at all times we are accommodating all young people as they learn and grow, so that they can make the most of their talents and their abilities. Accommodations are about helping people identify their strengths, their talents, their abilities, and helping them maximize those positive attributes of themselves so that they can set and reach challenging goals.

We want to help students become more aware of their own strengths and talents and abilities. But by the age of ten, through the process of public education, most people have become sensitive to their weaknesses and their inabilities. Most people learn some sense of shame and failure as they pass through the educational system. This is particularly true if a child has special needs. When a person believes that they are inadequate that belief becomes the worst barrier preventing their ultimate success.

Children with disabilities and their parents have often been told things such as that the child is "two standard deviations behind the norm" in critical areas. Everyone is well aware of what others say about what they *can't do*. Our goal as competent professionals is to help people become aware of what they *can do*, what they are good at, and what their talents and their abilities are. That way we encourage people to set high goals for their lives in all areas: social, work and education.

At the same time, the student needs to take the lead in planning for employment, because the student will not be motivated to succeed unless that student feels connected to the process of planning. If it is done *to them* it becomes punishing.

Remember reading in Chapter 1 about the young woman whose staff member said about her – "We did a person-centered plan but she still overeats." ? When we hear a statement like that, it is clear that the plan belongs to someone else other than the person. In educational settings we often find children who seem *permanently punished.*

A Word About Punishment

I've seen children strapped to their chairs because they won't sit still. I've seen children put in cardboard boxes as a timeout because they won't sit quietly as long as others can see them. I've seen children locked in closets and I've seen children who spend more time outside the classroom in a punishment chair in the hallway than inside the classroom week-to-week. Punishments diminish the child's sense of being a partner with their educators and a self-motivated learner who will learn to have the self-confidence they will need to succeed in their working lives.

The child needs to be at the center of the planning process in order for that plan to make sense to the child, and in order for the child to be motivated to do the hard work necessary to succeed at it.

Whatever goal the student has identified is the very first one that should be addressed. If adults plan in this fashion starting from when a student is a three-year-old, the child will be a highly motivated learner, who works hard, trusts others does well and succeeds, rather than a student who must be punished.

Put the Person First

The problems we observed in educational planning are replicated in employment planning throughout the life stages. Career counselors, job coaches and educators often look for a job that "somebody with disability X can do". For example, they mistakenly ask the question, *"What work can a blind person do?"* That is the wrong question and readers who have been paying attention know what the mistake is: we should look at what a person is interested in doing. We should match the interest of the person with their strengths and abilities, and then find a type of job that would meet those criteria. The correct question to ask is, *"What work would you like to prepare to do?"*

To ask the other way- with a focus on the disability first- is to focus on the barriers rather than the person. Put the person first in all planning processes. Look at the strengths, talents, desires and preferences of the person. Our goal is to assist people as they explore the potential of their future and help them prepare to realize their own dreams. Therefore, first step in employment preparation is to understand the person's dream; and the second step is to help the person figure out what actions they need to take to make their dream a reality.

The sky is the limit. Workers are limited only by their imagination, and that of the people who are helping them. Listen to what the person's goal is and then figure out what he or she needs to do to remove barriers to success.

No one is born knowing how to get through life. All of us have to undergo a process of trial and error everyday, to see what works for us. It takes some time for a person with a disability to learn how to manage their own special needs and remove the barriers from their pathway. This is not a process that people can do just once, and then move on. It is a "continuous quality improvement process" that must be engaged upon throughout life. The process involves first making a plan, giving it a try, discovering error through evaluation; and then regrouping and starting the cycle over again.

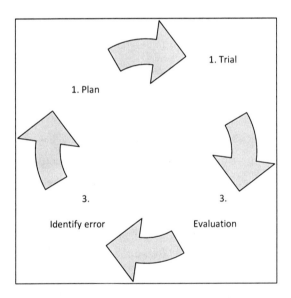

Figure 5: Continuous Improvement Cycle

People need to have to have multiple opportunities for trial and error; planning, evaluation and planning again so that they can learn what works for them and will help them become successful. People need the encouragement of others as they work their way through the process.

The Person-Centered Planning Questions:

The person centered career planning process starts with a self-exploration that arises from four questions:

1. What do I want to spend my time doing?

2. What is important to me?

3. What do I find difficult? (And/Or what do I want to avoid doing, which is just as important as what I do want to do.)

4. What do I already know how to do well?

These are the four questions that every student should answer and these are the four central questions in a person centered plan designed to facilitate transition from school-to-work.

Every job has specific tasks. After the person has identified the tasks or things they like to do (and don't like to do) by thinking through the questions above, the person may then match their self-assessment of interests, talents, the things they want to avoid, to the list of tasks that are part of any particular job. Job task lists are available on the internet or in a book on careers.

People should not lose heart if there is not a perfect match between their interests and a known job, because not all jobs come readymade. Job tasks can be shifted between jobs in a work place. Additionally, most people find that they can tolerate doing a few tasks that they don't like to do, if doing those tasks are a component of a job or role they highly value. Sometimes people find that they improve at a task by doing it, and they learn to like tasks they never expected to enjoy.

Planning In Action

Here is an example of this process in action. A young man who had a pronounced stutter wanted to have a job in which he would be in a leadership position. The position he wanted was a marketing job. Specifically, he wanted to  promote sales for his shop by giving a talk on the radio. The stutter had always been a serious communication barrier for this employee, but he competed strenuously to be the person selected to make the radio advertisement.

People were concerned that his radio spot would not go well. Some of them covered their self-interest by saying that they were worried that the employee's self-esteem would be damaged. Somehow the man was able to hang onto his assignment to make the audio advertisement. He was determined to do well.

After the advertising executives wrote the script, the young man memorized his speech and when the big day came, he gave that speech without a hitch. There was not one stutter in the entire communication. His voice was low-toned and pleasant to hear. Everyone was impressed with his ability to do a high quality audio spot.

That occurred several years ago, and that young man now works as a disc jockey. He still stutters sometimes in his one-on-one communication in informal settings but he never stutters on the radio.

Generally speaking, it's not for the best to put someone in a position where they have to use an emerging skill under high pressure conditions. However, there is always that time when what a person really wants to do is something (something that others do not believe he or she does well) when it is worth the risk of failure. It is best by far to let the person lead the way. If they want to give a task a try, why not? When people are highly motivated it is amazing what they can do to succeed.

When a person states their dream, their goal, it is up to everyone on their planning team to assure that all possible barriers to their success are removed. We can make physical accommodations fairly easily by turning the furniture to allow space for a wheelchair. We can print the materials in Braille or provide an online spoken format for printed materials. When necessary material can be read aloud onto a tape for a non-reading employee. When necessary we can set up accessible computers, monitors or keyboards. Where there is a will, there is a way.

Remember Amie from Chapter 1, the girl who loved Pizza? She now builds the carryout boxes for her Pizza restaurant. She knows exactly what her responsibilities are and works very, very efficiently. Amie's boss reports that Amie still takes as much care with each napkin she folds as if it were the first time.

The Measure of a Successful Human Being

Those of you who have studied Psychology probably know what Freud says about success in adult life. Freud said, "If you can love and you can work, then you are a successful adult."

That's an important thing to keep in mind when you are supporting someone in the area of employment.

Chapter 5 Thought Questions

1. What if you are a member of a planning team with someone who is interested in and has a talent for preparing food, for serving food, for being friendly to customers, keeping their hands clean and they are very accurate at measuring but they have not yet mastered how to count money, how to make change, what should you do?

2. When you review an IEP transition plan, how can you tell if the student was at the center of the planning process.

3. What would you respond if a co-worker asked you to help them place a person in a job, and started by asking you if you know what kinds of job a Blind person can do?

CHAPTER 6: Supporting Others In Building And Maintaining Relationships

"Love Is the Finest Thing Around"

As the poet once said, no one has any doubt that love is the finest thing around[27]. Finding love, keeping love and losing love are the key concerns in popular song, opera, movies, books, and even personal conversations. With all the effort going into the topic  even a casual observer can clearly see that there must be many difficulties in the process of finding and keeping a *significant other*, or there would not be nearly so much to say about it.

When we listen carefully to the words of popular love songs they can be categorized in the following ways:

1. Attraction: mostly addressing important topics like the way a person looks

2. Getting together: how it makes the singer feel to kiss someone, promises made

3. Keeping the loved one: warning others away, or trying to solve problems

---

[27] James Taylor song, *"Goin' To Carolina"*.

4. Mourning a lost love: trying to rekindle the romance or commenting on how one is suffering the permanence of the loss

Most songs tell a story about love at first sight. People just don't seem to write songs about the hard work of individual development through the life stages that lead to success in couples' relationships, which is how real love stories are maintained. Maintenance is important: what is the use of a "forever love" that falls apart when it is challenged?

Maybe reality is left out of love songs because it would be too hard to find a good rhyme for "satisfactory life stage completion". But at the root of every real love story is the dynamic process of two individuals who struggle to address the daily challenges of life in such a way that they are each able to meet their own needs while lending a helping hand to the other.

The success or failure of interpersonal relationships can be directly traced to the history of success or failure achieved by each of the partners as they grew up and sequentially addressed each of their own life stage developmental tasks. Erikkson's Psychosocial Stages[28] may be the clearest way to conceptualize the impact childhood events have on adult relationships.

---

[28] Erik Erikkson:

Erikkson's Psychosocial Stages

Erikkson identified eight stages of life: Infancy, Toddlers, Preschoolers, Elementary age students, Adolescence, Young Adulthood, Middle Age, and Old Age. For each of these age ranges, which he called by the term "Life Stages", Erikkson identified developmental tasks that had to be addressed by every person within each of the life stages, one age level after the other.

For example, just as most infants learn to sit at about the same time or within a few months of each other; and the same way they sequentially learn to pull up on furniture within a few months of each other and begin to craw within a few months of each other; infants are also developing cognitively and emotionally as well as physically.

Within a few months of each other all "typically developing" infants learn to smile, make eye contact, say simple words and grasp objects in the hand to bring to their mouth. These developmental tasks are clearly visible to any observer and they are well-recognized as developmental milestones, across cultures.

Erikkson built upon these "external" and observable

developmental features and identified ways in which infants
are developing in their hearts and minds, as well. The internal
life of an infant is not passive. Within the time span of a few
months after birth, infants are actively observing their world
and reaching a conclusion about whether or not the world into
which they were born is a safe world; one in which they are
likely to be able to trust others to meet their needs.

Trust versus Mistrust (Birth to age 1)

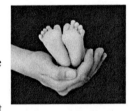

The infant aged birth to twelve months
is not able to express this process in
words, so adults who care for the child are
not able to mediate the opinion the infant
is developing about life by talking it about
it with him or her. At a very young an age the infant can not
understand what we say. The infant does all she or he can do
to make sense of life. That is, is to carefully observe each of
our actions. If the infant cries and we hurry to pick her up with
gentle hands and a friendly smile, she will develop trust. If
every time the infant cries with hunger she observes that we
hurry to feed her a warm and satisfying meal, she will develop
trust. If the infant frets with boredom and we entertain her, if
we keep her safe from things she fears, if the same loving adult
is almost always there with her, and if we follow a reliable day
to day schedule she can grow familiar with and count on, she
will learn to trust.

However, things can go quite differently, too.

If, for example, the infant lives in a home in which the daily life characterized by chaos; or if he or she is fed poor quality liquids (like soda) which leave her hungry; or if the infant is often physically uncomfortable; has multiple caregivers; or if he or she is not protected from things the infant fears (whether the fear is based upon something actually dangerous or not); then the person will develop serious doubts about the trustworthiness of adults in her world. The child will develop mistrust of those around her based on learning from the care the infant received early in life that people are not safe. Early care-giving failures to support the child emotionally create a breach of the security of the person's position in the world and of life itself, for the rest of the person's life.

Trust and mistrust are two polar ends of the same continuous line (or continuum). The continuum is a slippery scale, and most people slide back and forth a bit along that line, keeping mainly to somewhere in the center.

None of us have perfect trust in anyone, because we learned that people will let us down, when we have sometimes been let down. However, people who have lived in trustworthy families who performed their duties well enough that the infant was able to meet this first developmental task successfully, usually trust others well enough to form friendships in childhood, affiliations in adolescence, and develop a satisfying intimate relationship as an adult.

However, no single life stage stands alone as the litmus test of future positive relationship outcomes. Progress made through the developmental demands of next few life stages also impact the ability of the developing person to form a lasting love relationship, as well.

Let's look at a chart that shows each life stage and its developmental task before exploring the remaining life stages in detail.

Table 13: Erikkson's Developmental Life Stages

Stage	Age Range	Developmental Task
Trust Versus Mistrust	Birth to 24 Months	Determine if the world we are born into will be able to meet our needs or if we will not be able to count on others to come through for us.
Autonomy Versus Shame and Doubt	Age 2	Learning how to get what one wants without making others angry.
Initiative Versus	Ages 3 - 5 Years	Developing the

Guilt		ability to independently plan and carry out activities without failing to plan for how to deal with things that go wrong.
Industry Versus Inferiority	Ages 6 – 11 Years	Learning to compare our abilities to others' abilities without becoming conceited or depressed. Being able to continue to work hard for success even if others find success more easily.
Identity Versus Role Confusion	Ages 12 – 18 Years	Developing meaningful affiliation with a peer group and a close and lasting friendship with an individual.

Intimacy Versus Isolation	Ages 19 – 35 Years	Development of a reciprocal intimate relationship with another.
Generativity Versus Stagnation	Ages 35 – 55 Years	Self identification of a way that one can contribute to society and working to guide the next generation.
Integrity Versus Despair	Ages 56 and older	Acceptance of one's own life passage without bitterness for missed opportunities. Awareness and appreciation for one's own efforts and contributions to society.

Each life stage has its unique type of work that needs to be accomplished. Oddly enough, although everyone spends most of their time working at the task, people are largely unaware that they are engaged in a process that is anything but personal and unique. While each person believes that their concerns are

secret and "especially theirs", we must all address the very
same issues at about the same time, as we grow up through
childhood.

The process does not stop in adulthood, in fact, but life continues to
present standard developmental challenges to every person as they pass
through the life stages, one after the other right up to the end of life.

Fortunately, people are forced to re-address each of the previous life
challenges as they grow older. For example, if a person was not able to
establish much trust in others in infancy because their parents were too
immature to meet the needs of an infant, they may have a kind teacher
in elementary school, or a loving friend in adolescence that will help
them learn to trust. So the tasks can be successfully completed at any
time during life. Many people overcome the barriers of the less than
adequate parenting they received in infancy and childhood.

One of the most important outcomes of learning about developmental
stages is that is helps to make our own actions as adults, and the
actions of those around us, more predictable and understandable. If you
realize that a two year old is in a life stage in which they are trying to
learn how to meet their own needs (their need is to be in control)
without making everyone else angry, it helps you not to become angry
when they shout, "NO" frequently. If you realize that the two year old
must learn how to take control successfully to meet their
developmental task, as a mature parent or teacher the adult can

routinely provide a wide array of safe choices for two year olds that help them learn "how it's done".

A second outcome of learning about developmental stages is that when we look back at our past with a clear understanding of our needs at each stage, we are able to see ways in which some of the adults in our own lives unwittingly made it difficult for us to reach developmental goals. Once we understand what we needed to do, and compare it to what we were able to do, we are on our way to correcting the mistakes of the past and learning how to meet those unfinished developmental challenges of the past in our own present, and to support the pathway of development for others.

We have discussed the first life stage, *Trust versus Mistrust* above. The remaining eight life stages are to be described in the pages that follow.

Autonomy *versus* Shame and Doubt (1 -2 Years)

At the age of two years people struggle with the issue of power for the first time. Power relations form the underpinning of most of our  lives after this stage, and we are therefore tasked with discovering how we might best get our own way without making others angry at us. Since this task is routinely faced by all people when they are aged two years, it would seem quite clear that adults should focus child-raising at this age on teaching two year olds how to manage this. Instead, most parents and caregivers make this stage a battleground. They "blame the victim" by calling the age "The Terrible Twos", when actually it is lack of skill in parenting that creates the battle.

Adults can help two year olds meet their developmental task by providing a secure routine for them that is based upon their need for frequent feeding, afternoon naps, early awakening in the morning, and interesting, fun, creative and messy play.

The schedule needed by toddlers is quite different from an adult schedule, but it is critical to the development of healthy, active, friendly, self-assured and helpful toddlers. Toddlers cannot have meals served late, it makes them so irritable that they scream. Toddlers cannot be walked past cookies in the bakery section of the grocery store when they are hungry for lunch, they can not understand what you mean by "later". Toddlers simply cannot shop all day or stay out late at night the way adults can. They cannot sit in the car seat and the stroller indefinitely. Mature adults must be able to defer their own preferred schedule and desires for the few years that are needed to bring up a healthy child. This is what is meant by the term "maturity". Maturity is expected of adults, not of two year olds.

Parents can do so much to help their children develop into self-assured and helpful people who are fun to be around. Toddlerhood is the age children need to learn by experience about mud, rain puddles, sand, splashing water, and their own body. They need to taste, touch, smell, hear and see everything up close. By providing a safe time for the child to engage in messy activities every day (running through the sprinkler, splashing in a pool, playing in wet sand and learning to make cookies) the parent relieves the child of having to find messy things to do on their own.

Additionally, the parent can routinely ask the child, "What story book would you like me to read to you?"; "What game would you like me to play with you?"; "Would you like to go to the park now or to the library?"

Good choices are NOT wide open, such as: "What would you like to do?" And they are NOT closed, "You would like to eat macaroni now, wouldn't you?"

Real options given to toddlers that allow them to make meaningful choices between two or three good options allow a child to seize control in a positive manner. They teach the child how *good leadership* is managed. Good leadership is expected of the adult, not of a two year old.

It is also helpful if the parent is mature enough to be a kind and likeable guide for the child; helping the child explore while setting clear guidelines for safety. For example, a two year old needs to jump. A wise parent can say, "Yes, Johnny, jumping is fun! We jump here on the floor. We don't jump on the bed. Look, your teddy bear likes jumping on the floor with you!" Did you notice the parent did not have to shout, "No!" to stop Johnny from jumping on the bed? She just provided an explanation of where jumping can occur, and then she made it sound fun to follow the rules by demonstrating that the teddy bear was having fun jumping in the right way. Children who shout, "No!" are children who have "No!" shouted at them.

A two year old child with older siblings may seldom have the chance to successfully manage this stage, since inexperienced parents tend to always allow the elder child, usually a four to six year old who speaks more clearly and whom they know better, to make all of the decisions. Such parents cannot see the damage that they are doing, and it is probably similar to what was done to them by their own parents years earlier.

When parents are not calm and relaxed about parenting, when parents are unable to establish a child-friendly routine, when parents are afraid of letting a child play safely in messy ways, the two year old child in their care has trouble meeting their developmental task of learning to take control without making others angry. In fact, they raise a toddler who becomes an angry child.

An angry child is then thwarted at every turn because he or she is disagreeable. The angry child is shamed by the parent, who does not know why "the twos have to be so terrible." Instead of learning to be autonomous, the toddler who is not routinely given meaningful choice

207

that occurs over and over again during a daily, "child-friendly schedule" learns to doubt himself or herself through being shamed.

Fortunately, the issue of autonomy arises again in the next two stages as a "side issue" to the critical task required over those years and everyone gets a second chance to learn how to get what they want without making others angry. If the need to learn how to get ones way without making people angry is not learned in young childhood, the resulting teenager is very difficult to have around.

Initiative *versus* Guilt (3 – 5 Years)

A three to five year old child is tasked with learning how to set and carry out meaningful goals. Have you heard the phrase, "play is child's work"? The work of the three to five year old child is to play well with others.

Children need to be provided with interesting materials that they can determine how to use. For example a good experience for children is to be allowed set up a play living area such as a "house" created by dropping a sheet over a table, or setting out a tea party in the back yard using flowers and mud as the "food".

Children need to learn to take turns with the one tricycle and share the ball by throwing it to each other. They must take turns on the swings, and take turns at the sink when washing their hands before eating. Children of this age also need a firm routine, they need to know "what's next", what is expected of them, and how to perform well so that the adults in their lives are pleased with them.

At this age children who have a nice smile, speak clearly and those who have good ideas are highly sought after as playmates. However, if children refuse to share or if they lose their temper when they don't get their way, they will be left out of the play by the other children.

As you can imagine a "trusting" three to five year old child who, in the 2 year old stage, learned to take control in such a way that others were not made angry, has a strong advantage over a child who is still angry about their the lack of power to get what they need from their family.

Preschool teachers and busy parents often exacerbate problems that have already developed prior to this stage, by tending to favor children who have excelled at meeting their early goals. For example, children who already have excelled at the first two developmental tasks appear to be relaxed, friendly and cooperative. So it is not surprising that these are the very children most often selected by adults to lead the other children in line, or pass out the classroom snacks. This means that those children who are already doing well continue to be given a additional natural advantage over the rest of the classroom of children who are all working toward the same goals of the current stage.

On the other hand, those children who are more mistrustful than average because their early needs were not met, and those who doubt their abilities after their harsh experiences in the toddler years, now are more likely to fail at this stage, as well. The danger is for them to develop guilt because, in an effort to succeed in this stage (which is learning to plan and carry out their own goals), they inadvertently interfere with adult plans for the group.

Children who are awkward about finding ways to plan and carry out their own goals appear to be mischievous or naughty. They are frequently punished by the very adults they wanted so much to please, but since it is clear that they meant to please the adult, the adult will continue to act warmly towards them. These children learn to act naughty in a cute way, and may even learn to identify with the role of the "cute-naughty" one, and eventually develop a lasting interpersonal relationship style that will bring disappointment and hardship into their lives.

Alternately, some children have an instinctive understanding that the deck has been stacked against them from the start. This group of children may develop a righteous anger against adults for what appears to be the unfair treatment they receive. If left to develop anger can result in some children becoming bullies, while others simply create havoc every where they go. Both types of responses are maladaptive – meaning that they will not work out well for the child. Angry children are often labeled "troublemakers", and they frequently learn to identify with this label as if it were the only option possible for them, never realizing that if only their situation had allowed their early needs to be met they would not have to struggle now for mastery of the tasks required at this life stage.

This, however, does not mean that children who were less well served by caregivers in infancy and toddlerhood will never be able to reach parity with their peers, because creative children with high intelligence have ideas that attract other children. If conditions allow it at their school or social setting bright children can learn how to create plans and carry them out in the school setting.

Some children who were not able to trust adults in their early years do find it possible to develop greater trust and greater autonomy during the ages of three to five years, because they are able to learn to trust a teacher, their classmates and peers, and to trust their own initiative. If they are not able to extend the trust they now feel towards other children to the new adults in their school lives, these children are the ones who develop a mistrust of authority while getting along well with peers.

Child development is a unique art, and each child develops somewhat uniquely. There are some common developmental patterns that can help us identify and correct lagging development when we find it in the classroom.

When we observe that a child who was not successfully supported at home during the infancy and toddlerhood stages to develop trust and autonomy, we can assist the child by helping them learn to use their ideas and talents in a positive way during the three to five year old stage of pre-school and pre-work. They can learn to perform. However, if the teachers and other adults active in their lives between the ages of three and five are not able to help them "catch up" in developing trust and autonomy, the children may well assume a mistaken self-identity as a troublemaker that can only lead them into greater unhappiness as the years go forward.

Industry *versus* Inferiority (6 – 12 Years)

The stage of *industry versus inferiority* takes place during elementary school when children are between the ages of six and twelve years. This is a relatively stable time in the psychosocial lives of most children.

The primary task of this age range is for the child to learn how to work with a will. Children learn to compare the results of their work to the results earned by peers, and to cheerfully accept that while some of their work might be the best, it is also acceptable that the quality of the work of others sometimes far surpasses the quality of their own work. Perhaps the most important outcome in this stage is the awareness that one should seek to attain a "personal best", that is: to set a personal goal and then compare one's progress against one's own internal goal rather than comparing one's results against those of another.

Children at this stage need to learn enjoy work simply for the pleasure the activity brings as well as for the recognition that it brings. Both parents and teachers throw themselves into helping children attain these goals and this is the age at which children are given piano lessons, go to soccer camp, sing in the choir, and join Scouts in a general effort to help them develop their talents in a wide range of academic, social and physical arenas.

The key to success at this stage is fairly simple: children need to learn that despite the fact that others may be better at a task, they should continue to set personal goals for improvement and enjoy themselves as they work on building skills in a wide range of areas. If they learn that, then they have succeeded in meeting this developmental task.

Identify *versus* Role Confusion (13 – 19 Years)

After the calm of the previous six years, adolescence is again a time of rapid physical growth and turbulent emotional growth. The developmental task of *Identity versus Role Confusion* is for teenagers (aged 13 to 19 years) to learn who they identify with and to try out various roles before settling on an adult identity; and to achieve affiliation with a peer group that is meaningful to them.

Finding one's role is difficult work and it dredges up the old familiar issues of *trust versus mistrust, autonomy versus shame and doubt,* and *initiative versus guilt.* It is easy to see that a happy and trustful infant, a person who was given lots of assistance in learning how to make his or her autonomy palatable to those around him or her was off to a good start. If that was followed by becoming a leader in preschool settings among peers and by recognition by teachers in elementary school ready, the child was well prepared to cheerfully address skill building in academic and social arenas- will also enter this new stage in the best possible frame of mind.

These are the very teenagers who succeed in pleasing adults and other teens their age. They run the school newspaper, star on the sports team and win scholarships.

The task is not easy for children who were not able to make a good adjustment at any of the previous life stages.

Those parents who did not like to see autonomy develop in infancy are going to like autonomy in adolescents even less. Those parents will use the same tactics of *shame* to control the teenager's attempt to be self sufficient, with the same result: *more doubt* of self.

A teenager who doubts their own worth is ill prepared for the often cruel and frightening task of finding acceptance in a clique, and such a child may well be relegated to joining a group at the bottom of the popularity ranking. Joining one or another group is unavoidable, but there is a high cost in joining a low ranking group. Such a group is aware of the shame attached to their rank, and they often try to show in every way from clothing, to hair, music, makeup, and jewelry that they "don't care" about being accepted. They would like others to believe that they have, in fact, already rejected the more popular groups and chosen this one for their affiliation.

This scenario could have been avoided by parents if they had been able to accept that their job – from day one- was to prepare their children to be successful adults; not to keep their children from having a single independent thought, or from ever making a mess or a mistake.

Adolescents with low autonomy and high self-doubt may not always go so far as to join a "counter popular" group in adolescence. Some may just "go along with the gang" so that they do not have to make any decisions on their own, or come to anyone's notice. Adolescents who have learned that they are not allowed to be autonomous may become or marry abusive partners, or become or marry bullies who need a scapegoat to blame for their own feelings of inadequacy or anger.

Teenagers who failed to develop trust in their parents, teachers or peers may withdraw and sequester themselves as much as possible in

215

an "alternate world" composed of books, science fiction, computers, sports or the arts. Being good at reading or writing, computers, sports or the arts is not the same as being sequestered in them. A person with a talent will appropriately put a lot of time into effort toward developing that talent greatly in adolescence, but they will also have friends, attend family outings cheerfully and find ways to contribute to those in society more needy than themselves.

Adolescents who are working successfully toward meeting their developmental goals will try out for several school events (such as drill team, marching band, or a musical) but they will also maintain their older, deeper friendships while finding new friends in their larger school setting. They will fall in and out of love a number of times, and have crushes on young teachers, coaches, and movie and recording stars. They will try to dress in the latest fashion, as far as their budget allows, and fix their hair the same way the popular kids in school wear theirs. Both genders often try to excel at sports to gain respect from peers and adults, and everyone at this age seeks self-sufficiency (except in financial matters) from their parents who should take this storm of trial and error with good humor and who should cheerfully let adolescent demands and accusations roll off their back like water.

Parents can greatly help their adolescents meet the developmental stage by showing interest in what their child wants to talk about, coming to their school to see them perform, reviewing their homework and sharing outside interests (such as attending the symphony) with

216

them. Home needs to be a safe haven for adolescents and parents can help them by forbidding their teenagers from being away from home seven days a week, and at all hours of the night. Family activities are crucial for a good transition to adulthood and they give teenagers a break from having to be in top form at all times.

But that said, adolescents must learn to try their wings. Adolescents should choose their friends, choose the clubs to which they belong and, as far as possible choose their clothing so that they can "try on" various adult-type identities and learn which will work best for them. Most of all, adolescents need to affiliate with a group, and parents should go to great lengths to have snacks and treats available at all times for their children's friends and to welcome all of their child's peers to the house on a regular basis. Parents need to meet the parents of their child's friends and assure that if the rules are different from home to home, that one's own child is well prepared to follow the guidance of their parents in dealing with these differences.

Setting guidelines for adolescents with clear and un-shifting consequences helps young people meet the demands of this very intense life stage.

Intimacy *versus* Isolation (20 – 35 years)

As adolescents move into young adulthood there is some blending of the developmental tasks between the completion of the *affiliation* tasks of the previous life

217

stage and the early years of the new life stage, which calls for the formation of a reciprocal intimate relationship and learning how to compromise gracefully.

As one can imagine if a person has not adequately found acceptance within a social group with whom they want to affiliate in adolescence, young adults may be stuck slavishly copying the outward signs of group membership to disguise their lack of acceptance.

Many times families move from one town to another when their children are in the stage in which affiliation is the key to emotional growth and stability, and the children find it difficult or impossible to make the shift from one set of expectations to another quickly enough to be absorbed into an acceptable group in the new setting. In such cases if the adolescent had met earlier developmental tasks well enough, a short period of time devoted to affiliation in the early years of the stage for *Intimacy versus Isolation* will suffice and then they are prepared to move forward toward establishing intimacy with a significant other.

The term "intimacy" as used here, includes sexual intimacy, but extends far beyond the level of biological need, to include an exchange of deeply held thoughts, beliefs, goals and hopes with a loved one who reflects ones own caring, support and devotion back to one. That the relationship must be reciprocal is a given.

It is clear that at this stage an individual who has not learned to *trust* will face great difficulty in establishing a truly intimate relationship with a life partner. If one has not learned how to be *self-sufficient and autonomous*, he or she will have difficulty being a true partner to an adult relationship, and instead this person will tend to "second guess" the loved one, always expecting to be hurt, rejected or punished while secretly hoping that "this time it will work out ok". In fact, a person who does not trust and is not self-sufficient will often seek another of the same emotional level and one of the pair will begin to serve as the bully, over time, while the other will serve as the scapegoat.

People do not do these things on purpose. We are driven by ideas we believe so deeply that we don't even notice them. Since we don't notice them we can't question them and we simply go through life making decisions and taking actions that seem "right" to us in some way, but which are really not in our best interest. And we never know why.

Sometimes people who do not have enough trust in others or belief in their own self- sufficiency to establish an intimate relationship will seek refuge in affiliation with others whom they believe are even less advantaged than they are, themselves. Then, within this group at least, they feel that they are competent and successful. If they met the developmental stage of *Industry versus Inferiority* successfully, then they may be employed for many years in one setting. If they have failed to develop self-sufficiency they may sometimes allow the "bully" side of their character surface in their work, even though they

219

don't like that side of themselves. When people find themselves in this situation they can grow.

It is never too late to successfully complete any of the developmental tasks, and, in fact, many people who have struggled the hardest for these gains make the best teachers and can guide many others to success.

Generativity *versus* Stagnation (36 to 55 Years)

Generativity begins at the very point at which we left off in our discussion of the previous stage, *Intimacy versus Isolation*. As people pass through the life stages they accumulate wisdom. Wanting to share their wisdom, or what they have learned with others, for the benefit of others, is an excellent way to define the word "generativity".

As we settle into our lives, when the main uncertainties such as "Who am I?" and "How can I support myself?" and "Who shall I love?" are settled, people are free to work on the less urgent questions of life. For some, the most important remaining question is: "What is the meaning of life?" and they come to the conclusion that one of the main goals in life should be to help others. Most people draw a conclusion something like this during their working decades and before retirement, and these people make a widespread difference in our society though their tireless work with disadvantaged people and underserved groups.

It is also during the years after a person reaches the age of 50 that they begin to think back over their life and readdress any unresolved life stage issues that they can identify. As their parents enter old age and then pass away, many people are able to forgive their parents for the early pain they endured because they now understand how difficult child rearing is, and they realize that their parents were also often carrying out the same treatment that they received from their own parents.

People also look back over their own actions through the years and identify situations in which they believe they could have done better. This is a helpful exercise for them, and it prepares people for entering the next stage with the beginning skills they will need to develop the characteristic "long distance" view of life that make the elders and leaders of our society so wise.

Integrity *versus* Despair ("56 Years" and Older)

Over the decades since the theory was first published, people have learned to age more slowly. Better diet, more advanced medical care, more leisure time and a greater sense of a need to self actualize have made age 60 the "new 45". (That's my story and I am sticking to it!) While the ages and dates attached to each stage may have changed over time, the life stages related to retirement years remain the same. During the retirement years people face their own mortality. The physical effects of aging cannot be ignored, and a person's gradually becomes aware that over the course of the years more of their older relatives and friends pass away with regularity.

At this time of life a person must learn how to review their personal life story and draw conclusions about their life passage. As difficult as certain events and episodes of life have been for most of us, when we reach our sixties and seventies we are reassured that despite the hardships we have faced, we have done fairly well, all in all.

Most people develop a sense of their life story as a happy one. They relish the high points, they revel in the exciting points, and they are proud of the steadfast way they faced adversity.

Most people report that they view their greatest accomplishment to be providing for a family and raising their children to contribute to society. As they enter their nineties most of their family members, siblings, parents, aunts and uncles and cousins have passed on. Then death no longer seems frightening but appears to be the next frontier, or at least, it has been reportedly viewed by most elders as an accepted end to this life.

Now, On To Romance

The discussion we have just had concerning life  stages was a necessary precursor to the discussion everyone has been waiting for. Before we can address romance and supporting people as they seek their soul mate, we have to understand the predictable challenges that all people face as they pass through the life stages on the way to the appropriate age at which the search for a husband or wife becomes the most important issue in people's lives.

If we did not take the time to learn about the challenges at each life stage, then we would nt be able to understand why people act as they do. We need this understanding so we can support people in learning how to resolve old issues in the areas of trust / mistrust or self-sufficiency versus self-doubt, so that they can move forward in healthy ways.

Building Relationships That Last

Despite the messages about falling in love at first sight that we all know from popular music, there is no magic about falling in love. Everyone stays the same person that they were before, whether they have a relationship or not. Some of our characteristics are loveable and would easily lead to a long-term happy relationship, while others among our characteristics would create problems in a relationship and cause a break up.

That is why in order to build a long lasting relationship people have to go to the trouble of learning who they are (and why), and learning what it is that they most want out of life. If we find that our habits are destructive we may be interested in making the personal changes in thought and deed that would lead to long term happiness with another person. Of course it doesn't hurt if we can learn how to "work things out" with others along the way, as well.

A love affair can only succeed when each person in the relationship works on taking care of the individual growth that will teach them how to be a good life partner for the other.

To help someone *discover themselves*, that is, to learn what they actually believe about themselves and to learn how that belief might impact a potential love-relationship, there are a series of questions they can consider. There are NOT any right answers to any of these questions, nor is there a wrong answer.

What is valuable about the exercise for people is the opportunity to start off on the road to self discovery that these questions initiate. The following questions are from a workshop jointly written and presented in 1999 by Anita Carroll, a People First leader who also was a VISTA,[29] and Tanya Whitehead, her People First Advisor and friend.

Question 1: Make a list of what you want from a boyfriend or a girlfriend or spouse.

In workshops when this question is asked people often list a set of characteristics like "friendship, someone to talk to, someone to help out, honesty, someone beautiful, someone rich, someone like me, or someone who shares". What we have never heard in a workshop is an answer that indicates the person is aware that the *other* person in relationship also has a list of "desirables" and that the matching up of those two lists is a key to the survival of the relationship.

As we start seeking a love relationship we are aware that we have not listed all of the things that we will eventually demand from others in an intimate relationship, and we may be aware that we do not even know what some of the things we want from others even are. So in addition to not knowing enough about what it is we actually want, and here is

---

[29] "Forever Yours" Anita Carroll & Tanya Whitehead, People First of Kansas City, Missouri

really dangerous part, *we don't know anything that is on the list of our potential loved one*, and so we can ruin that relationship without ever knowing why.

People reach out to each other, but they often do so from behind a barrier like a brick wall. We call to each other, dress for each other, flirt and enlist the help of others in trying to get the chosen person to fall in love with us; but we are really reaching out from behind a brick wall if we do not share our real self with the person we hope will learn to love us. We are often sending a message about what we wish we were, rather than who we really are.

To share ourselves we first have to learn what we really *are* like and then we must become comfortable with ourselves. Most people who undertake this process find that they have a lot of growing to do. Perhaps not surprisingly, people who know that they need to grow make the best life partners because they work the hardest at it.

Question 2: What makes you mad at your friends?

When this question is asked at a workshop, people list all kinds of things, such as: "if they lie to me, if they don't call me back, if they leave me out, if they don't share what they have."

It is very easy to think that the other person has made us angry, but the truth is that our feelings are within us and belong to us; and it is only we, ourselves, that control whether we feel angry or just disappointed.

When we do become angry, we do so because we have learned to treat others the way that we have been treated, rather than the way that we know people should be treated. As we know from studying Erikkson's Psychosocial Life Stages, our knowledge of how to act in our relationships starts in infancy. It is tempting to grow up to act exactly the way the adults in our early lives acted, but we do have a choice. Once we begin to think about it and search for the way we would like to think and feel and act, we have half the battle won.

When there is a disagreement it helps to follow these rules:
- Do not shout. Keep a low voice.
- Don't walk away.
- Listen to the other person and try to see what they mean.
- Try to think of a way to compromise.
- Show the other person that you appreciate the time and effort they spent listening to you.

Question 3: Who do you want to be?

Who do you want to be? It is rare, in workshops, to hear "I just want to be myself!" Most respondents say the name of a vocal recording artist or a movie star, or someone they know who is very popular and seems happy. It is helpful to people when they have a role model, because it

227

takes a long time and a lot of work to learn how to be the best person each of us can be. But we can not be a good partner in a relationship until we know who we really are and how we came to be that way. Then we can decide which way we want to grow.

A relationship comes with work that will need to be done by both of the people who are in that relationship. Both have to learn how to be a loyal friend; they have to learn to trust each other as well as to be trustworthy for the other. Both partners need to learn how to recognize their own anger and learn how to manage it. Both must learn to recognize and repent when they have hurt the other or done something wrong, so that they can correct the damage. Both have to learn to forgive the other. A lasting relationship is a lot of work. This is surely a big part of what it means to be an adult.

Question 4: Why aren't we talking about being in love?

We are!

An intimate relationship is part of your regular life, not part of a fairy tale. Getting through life has been pretty hard work so far, hasn't it? I don't see why we should assume that the hard work would stop once we find our soul mate.

Question 5: What do you want from a close friend?

In workshop settings people often say, "I want someone faithful, someone truthful, someone loving and kind, someone who won't pressure me, someone who does not gossip, someone I can trust."

These qualities are, indeed, some of the qualities that will make a good friend and a good spouse, but it goes both ways. If you want to have a friend or a spouse with these characteristics, you will have to learn how to develop the same characteristics within yourself so that you are a good friend and a good spouse, yourself.

Marriage will demand many things from you, including:

- generosity because sometimes you will have to share when there really was not enough for even one;
- self-control so that you keep your temper when it would be really easy to lose it;
- imagination: so that you can understand the feelings of the other; patience when the loved one is not the best they can be;
- trust in the loved one even after they have let you down; commitment to keep on growing and changing together so that your union will last a life time.

You can see, I am sure, that you can't count on a feeling like "being in love" to get you though all this. A successful relationship will take lots and lots of daily work.

229

Question 6: Which of the items listed below are reasons for a marriage that will stand the test of time and might lead to a long lasting marriage?	
• Want to share my life • Want companionship • Want sexual fulfillment • Want economic security & stability • Want to be part of a couple • Want social status of marriage • Want independence from parents • Want to be and have a best friend	• Want to be spoiled by someone • Want someone to be there whenever I want them • Want someone with me so I don't have to be alone • Want to be the head of a household and in charge • Want to make someone happy • Want to be needed

You may observe that most of the items listed on the right side of the table will not lead to a long and stable marriage, because they fail to consider the input coming from the other person in the partnership. You can only have a relationship that lasts with a person who is as important to you as you are to yourself.

Question 7: What comes along with marriage?

Among other things, marriage is a financial obligation and a legal commitment; it means more expenses and higher bills; it means less freedom since each partner in the marriage must always safeguard the interests of the other. Marriage means more laundry and more housework, but it also means that the chores can be shared between two people. Marriage means learning how to solve problems together. Marriage is a challenge, and long lasting marriages are a great achievement.

Planning with People Around Relationships

Group discussions are a very good way to work thorough these questions and issues, because being exposed to the ideas and insights of others improve the ability each of us has to understand the complex issues related to developing healthy and long lasting relationships.

Of course strict confidentiality is an absolute must because in a group of people learning together many sensitive thoughts and ideas are shared. It would be devastating to individuals if their comments were ever shared with anyone outside the group. This includes the staff NOT writing the group progress in the charts, and not gossiping with staff in regard to the comments shared within the group.

Good progress made in a group can include getting to know each other, learning that no one is perfect; finding that people have interests and hopes in common; that people share the same the same values and want to live the same way. Working in a group setting also lets people have practice in becoming the type of friend and partner they really want to be at heart.

Chapter Six Thought Questions

1. Briefly describe what you learned about life stages and their challenges.

2. Describe how you can use the information you learned about Erikkson in your own life.

3. How could you use the information you learned about supporting people in developing lasting intimate relationships?

CHAPTER 7: Doing the Ordinary, in an Extraordinary Way

<u>Supporting Others</u>

A great deal has been written about case management and human service professional roles from the perspective of the various disciplines (whether dentistry, medicine, nursing, social work, education or psychology). People who study this kind of thing know a lot of theory about behavior modification, reinforcement and sequential goals.

Similarly, much has been written about Person-Centered ideals in supports and services.

But there is a gap between the two literatures. This gap leaves the people who provide services and supports flailing around between rules on the one hand, on supportive person centered assistance on the other.

In Chapter 7 of this book, we will try to build a bridge across that gap so that human service specialists (that would be you) can see how to apply their extensive discipline specific knowledge about disability and group management within agency specific guidelines, <u>in a person centered way</u>. We will bring it all together.

To help us, we will review the history of case management and the traditional models of case management service. One of the models this chapter will demonstrate will show how service professionals can use a multidisciplinary (or "interprofessional") approach so that agencies can truly collaborate in the effort to provide the highest level of 21st Century client supports and services. Finally, we will review several self-assessment tools that caring professionals in the field can utilize to self evaluate their current level of expertise in the area, and independently set goals for personal and professional growth.

While the differences between the lives of people with and without disabilities is striking and those life style differences are the focus of all the attention, it can not be denied that the lives of all human beings are more similar than they are different.

Every person passes through each of the life stages discussed earlier. Each person has hopes and dreams, talents, and abilities that they would like to enhance. Everyone wants to be liked by others and appreciated, recognized and accepted; and everyone wants to have friends and family with whom they may share life's journey. Everyone believes that they have something of intrinsic value to offer others, and they want to do right by others.

The great wave of activity we see around us every day is evidence of the effort just about everybody is making to do just that- it is, as the French say, "life ordinaire".

Of course ordinary life doesn't always unfold so very simply and easily. Something is always breaking down – if it is not the garage door opener, it's the washing machine. We have arguments and fall out with our friends; sometimes we divorce our mates. Our beloved pets have life-cycles much shorter than ours, and our hearts are broken as they age and then die in what seems so short a time. We witness the gradual aging of our parents; and then quite unexpectedly our own bodies begin to show signs of aging and we have to seek medical care, perhaps taking medication on a daily basis for a chronic condition.

While people pass through the life stage *Intimacy versus Isolation*, between ages 20 and 55 years, people with and without a disability work, volunteer, join clubs, play sports, sometimes marry and might have children. We all contribute to society in many ways.

Since we all pass through the same life stages, and have the same needs and the same goals the question, *"what role must a disability play in life?"* almost asks itself.

It is true that the presence of a disability sometimes creates a barrier to doing things the ordinary way. Even if so, what is stopping people with disabilities from just going ahead and doing all these ordinary things in an extraordinary way? Nothing! They can!

History of Case Management

Prior to the 1960s it was typical for people with severe disabilities to be placed in institutions by their families or by the state. The deinstitutionalization movement of the 1960s was based on a new awareness of the importance of people living in the community. Since communities were largely unprepared to manage the needs of people coming out of institutions. From the earliest times the training for case workers and support persons had an emphasis on advocacy and normalization principles (Wolfensburger, 1972[30]).

While the ideal of community living began to win people's hearts, it took some time to establish community supports. In the short term, an increasing number of programs were developed to meet people's medical, financial, social and education needs. However, these programs were neither really based in the community nor were they easily accessible to potential users. Initially the daily work of service staff was to streamline the process by which individuals could access services and to integrate activities between agencies.

Over time, as legislation demanded it, the community improved its array of supports that make it possible for people to live fully in the community. The current focus of the service system is to deliver the

---

[30] Wolfsensberger, 1972

supports needed by people to them in the community from birth onward. However, as time has marched onward the perception of disability has undergone a radical change. No longer are people with disabilities viewed as incapable of working and contributing to society. Services and supports offered by the system now are seen as temporary aides offered to support a person as they reach self-sufficiency.

For those of us who worked in the disability service system throughout the entire time period from the 1950s to the present time, it has seemed to be a painfully slow transformation. But looking backward from the new millennium to the grim days of institutionalization, society has taken a gigantic leap and the "extraordinary" was accomplished by a wide variety of people who each did the best they could, given the constraints of their working conditions.

People now expect and anticipate a life lived fully and richly in the community, and it is due to the often exasperating effort of scores and scores of dedicated system employees who labored long and worked tirelessly under continually changing expectations and demands that such a transformation of expectations was possible. Hats off to you!

Traditional models of case management service

Over the years during which the efforts to provide supports in the community were growing, there were three basic designs by which system services were delivered, in turn.

These were:

1) The Role Focused Approach in which the primary goal was defined as an increased service employee accountability, efficiency and effectiveness;

2) The Resource Procurement Approach in which the primary goal was the provision of or mobilization of services to meet the needs of clients; and

3) The Client Empowerment Approach in which there was a radical change in the relationship between the service system and the individual and his or her family, leading to the empowerment of the client.

The "Role Focused" approach was heavily dependent upon the expertise of the service system employee to assess the client's areas of need (which were considered to be his or her "problems").

This included a staff responsibility to obtain or give a diagnosis to the client through an evaluation process and then to select what the service system employee believed were suitable services to help the

238

client overcome his or her "problems". There was extensive monitoring of the client's progress in meeting the goals set by the system employee, tracking to verify that the desired results were maintained, and accountability for the employee for assuring the client's met their annual goals and "overcame impediments".

This approach put the employee in the management seat, and usurped the individual's decision-making authority over what goals they would like to accomplish and what services they require to meet their self-defined needs.

In the "Resource Procurement" approach, the system employee served as a broker who organized community supports to meet the needs of clients, insures that the services are delivered to the client and motivates the client to improve in specified ways. This approach allows the client to help decide what needs he or she has, but assumes that the client is unable to assume the primary responsibility for goal setting and for selecting service providers. It did function to teach people who use services how to take on the role of self- determination, as the next stage in system services was reached.

Finally, the third approach is the "client empowerment" approach in which the individual is "enabled" to take an active or leadership role in the planning process and in decision-making. The role played by the system employee is to restore the individual's sense of competence so that he or she is able to set personal goals and arrange supports needed to establish a rich life in the community.

Sometimes system employees who have worked in the field over a long period of time find that the empowerment approach is challenging for them. The employee has to develop a proactive and anticipatory style that allows them to identify potential problems before they occur, so that crises can be avoided, while continuing to strongly believe in the right of the person and their family to self-determination. The employee must help create an environment in which experimentation and trial and error are acceptable events in people's lives.

In our daily work-lives we are aware that all three approaches are still around for the time being. But every year we make more progress toward a system that is flexible, responsive and respectful towards the people we serve. We do this by a process of self-examination designed to help us understand our own strengths and to identify areas in which we must improve. Below you will find the Support Person Checklist.

Support Person Checklist

The following questions are for you to ask yourself. To answer them you will have to put yourself "in the shoes" of someone you support.

Satisfaction:

- Would the person I support say that they are pleased with my work, in general?

- Would the person I support say that they feel good about working with me?
- Would the person I support say that they would recommend me to a friend who needed help?

Helpfulness:

- Would the person I support feel that I made things better or worse for them?

Accessibility:

- Would the person I support say that I respect them?
- Would the person I support say that I seem to like them?

Partnership:

- Do I truly agree with the goals set by the person I support most of the time?
- Do we discuss things together effectively?
- Do we agree about most important things?

After you have had the chance to answer the questions above, reflect for a few minutes on how it would feel to be the person you support (what if you were the person you are supporting?), and what would it be like to be supported by you. It is a good idea to put yourself in the

241

other's shoes, from time to time. It helps us to keep our work at the highest level, when we do.

Person Centered Self Assessment Tool For Support People

A People First State President and VISTA, one person, Anita Carroll, and her advisor prepared and delivered a national workshop called *"Reaching For the Stars"*[31] on the topic of setting and reaching personal goals. This training was helpful for both self-advocates and for support people.

We called the training, "Reaching for the Stars" because *stars* represent our idealized selves.

When we reach for the stars we are trying to catch a vision of who we want to be and what we want our life to be like. Maybe we think of stars as our ideal selves because our needs and our emotions are so earthy and primitive. Stars are clean and bright and beautiful, although

---

[31] Anita Carroll and Tanya Whitehead, Reach For The Stars, 1999 Workshop Presentation.

distant. They give us something greater than we currently are to wish upon and to reach for.

Keep it in mind, as you support people, that everyone wants to reach for the stars in their life. For over twenty-five years people with disabilities have been giving the system the same feedback: they have said that they want to choose their own homes in the community, choose their own staff and work in real settings.

People want to be self sufficient, capable and empowered. Those goals might be thought of as the star for which they are reaching. How close are they to having reached those stars? The answer depends upon the kind of support that they can get from you.

Below are a few questions designed to let people who support others with disabilities explore how we feel we are doing at supporting the people we work with, as they reach for their stars

> Question 1: Do we do things for others that they could do for themselves?

Professionals sometimes do things for people that people really should do for themselves. It is not surprising that sometimes staff want to take care of people. In fact, many were hired to do just that. However, it could be that staff sometimes make decisions for people that people should be able to make for themselves.

243

It is not good for people to depend on others to do the things that they can do for themselves. After a while they grow to expect others to take care of them, and then to demand it. People learn that if they don't take care of themselves, someone else will step forward and do it for them. At some point if we help someone too much, it changes from *helping them* to *hurting them*.

Question 2: Why do we feel driven to help others?

Some helpers have decided that they want to help others because they recall a time that they needed help, and could not get any. Others have said that they were helped too much by adults when they were younger and now they want to be the ones to "give back".

Whatever the reason might be, when we "over-help" others we send them a message that we don't believe they can manage things adequately on their own. When someone has been told throughout their lifetime that they are not capable of tasks, and when we take the task out of their hands, we encourage the people we actually wish to help to be their own worst enemy: we show them that they should believe they are incapable, too.

Sometimes when someone rejects the help of staff they are given a social punishment, such as the "silent treatment". When others observe this happening they learn to accept the situation as it is, rather than to try to reach for the stars.

Question 3: What keeps us "helpers" stuck?

Many staff are lifelong "helpers". When we were in Kindergarten we dried the tears of other children who felt abandoned on the first day of school, we were helpers. We knew how to empathize with them because we had felt abandoned at other times, ourselves. When we were in the Third Grade we shared our snacks with others, even though there was not really enough to go around. We were helpers. We shared whatever we had because there had been times we had watched others enjoy something in front of us, and we felt deprived.

We are people for whom "helping" is a way of life. It is our nature. However, it may be possible that we sometimes "over-help" or tell people what to do when we should not. Maybe it is because in the past we have faced danger alone, and the reminder of how helpless we felt in the past makes us feel anxious when someone else seems to be in the frightening and lonely position we know so well.

In order to grow, ourselves, we have to learn how to look into the reasons that underlie our helping nature.

One staff member suddenly realized that she was driven to help others because she was anxious about herself. When this realization hit her she wanted to change. She decided to spend at least some of her effort helping herself. So she sat down and made a rule for herself: she said, "Each time I realize that I have over-helped someone else I have to go home and do something extra that will help myself."

She realized that she had been cheated of receiving the help that she needed as a child, but no amount of over-helping the people around her in her adult life would ever make up for it.

She just had to accept that this is they way it is.

With some suggestions from others she was able to learn to "help herself" by doing things she would ordinarily consider too expensive or too time consuming (that is, things that would keep her from having the time to help someone else). By getting a professional pedicure, or a massage or going to a movie that she wanted to see every time she realized she had "over-helped" someone else, she broke the myth that kept her bound to a life of servitude. As she learned to care more for herself in the present day, she found she was able to step back and let other adults learn to meet their own needs, as well.

Question 4: What is it about yourself that you respect?

Chances are that you respect yourself, in part, because someone whom you respect seems to believe in you. That gives you confidence.

What if, instead of knowing that most people view disability and "differences" as bad, you had the unmistakable impression that most people believed that the differences between people were good things? It may be difficult to imagine how that such approval would feel, since most of society is so deeply mired in the belief that differences are quite bad things, indeed.

Most of the time we know that we are lucky when we have one or two people in our lives that believe in us, and truly support us. At times, we have no one. This is the lifelong situation of most people with severe disabilities.

When we find ourselves at a time when no one around us seems to respect us, we have to find a way to learn to believe in ourselves for the time being. It may take some practice to do this. Some have said that it helped them to accept that they were human. To be human is to be imperfect, but even though imperfect, to be of value.

Some staff people have promised themselves that they will provide honest respect to each of the people they work with, every day. Interestingly they have found that as they focused on respecting others,

247

they were increasingly respected by others, and their own self respect increased as well.

Chapter 7 Thought Questions

1. What are some of the new ideas you have gotten from reading this section on human services? How will you use the ideas in your daily life?

2. In what ways do people with disabilities depend upon others to help remove barriers so that they are not prohibited from full participation in the community?

3. How can people in the service system be of the most help to others?

CHAPTER 8: Accommodations from a Person-Centered Perspective

Ideas for Supporting People With Specific Disabilities

Every American is entitled to a free, public education. During their educational years all public school students are expected to be exposed to career awareness at one level or another, to prepare them to be contributing members of society in their adult years. Employers need good employees who will come in on time. They need employees who will learn the job, perform the job well, get along with others, follow whatever the laws are that apply, show concern for customers, and help make the business money.

In order to attend school and to prepare for and fill jobs, people with disabilities may need an array of tools to remove barriers from full participation.

While we want our behavior to consistently demonstrate our internal respect for people by focusing on their attributes, talents, abilities, interests, and preferences, it makes sense to have a binder filled with accommodation tools and techniques that people can utilize to remove barriers against their full participation. We respect the effort that will be needed to remove those barriers.

As you will remember from earlier in the book, American law compels educational institutions to offer reasonable accommodations to children who meet specific diagnostic criterion, as shown below.

COVERED DISABILITIES
1. Autism
2. Mental Retardation
3. Hearing Impairments
4. Deafness
5. Visual Impairments
6. Speech or Language Impairments
7. Serious Emotional Disturbances
8. Orthopedic Impairments
9. Traumatic Brain Injury
10. Specific Learning Disabilities
11. Other Health Impairments

We will take each of the covered disability types and explore some sorts of accommodations that might be useful to the student. Below this list of featured general practices, we will provide online resources for further exploration. In the Reference section, below, additional published materials will be listed for further reading.

Let's begin our exploration with a reminder that all of our work is done within a value-based common cultural context. We share a common respect for people (with and without disabilities). We see the whole person (from a strengths model) and put the person first, before the disability. Finally, we remember that people come from cultural subsets within America, each one of which holds dear a unique perspective on health and illness. It is necessary for people who want to work with others to understand these unique perspectives because the behaviors and preferences of the people with whom we are working only make sense in the light of their belief system. When we take the time to learn about a person's culture and we respect their spoken and inferred preferences based on their belief system, we can be considered Culturally Competent.

Cultural Competency

Here is an example of how one professional learned to become more culturally competent.

Dianne was a psychologist working in a busy university hospital in a large Midwestern city, as the psychologist on the Cleft Lip and Palate team. Dianne had served on the team for about four years when she was sent to do an 'intake' (or initial meeting) with a young couple who had just given birth to their first child, a boy with a cleft lip and palate.

Initial visits with new parents are very stressful for everyone. Most new parents are weeping. One or more grandmothers and aunts of the baby may be in the room and they are anxiously trying to comfort the new parents. Most American parents are aware of the issues that will be presented to their baby over the years by the clefting condition that include such aspects as: looking 'impaired' to the observer; having trouble with eating; frequent corrective surgeries; and the potential of learning problems.

Often the first question Americans ask the intake person is, "Why did this happen?" They want assurances that the "problem" can be fixed. They want to know if they can sue the doctor. Each parent fears that they did something wrong that caused the clefting condition. It can take months or even years for many parents to accept the situation and learn to make the best of it.

When Dianne entered this specific room for the first time she could feel a very different emotional current between the family members. There were no tears, no stress in evidence anywhere. The elderly uncle and grandmother gathered around the bed were smiling peacefully. The father appeared proud and while he sat across the room, he was beaming at his wife. The young mother, holding her newborn, was smiling with joy. Dianne checked the card to be sure she had entered the right room. Sure enough, this was the right case- and there was the newborn with a cleft of the lip and palate peeking out of the blanket in his mother's arms.

Dianne understood immediately that the family had a very different perspective on clefting than was usual in America.

Dianne knew that the person in power in the Hmong family was not the mother, but the elderly uncle. She greeted him directly, told him her name and nodded. The young father spoke for his uncle and returned the greeting. Uncle gestured toward the young mother and Dianne then approached the bed, greeting the young mother. While this was a different method of entering a conversation with a patient, Dianne knew that the young mother needed the approval of her husband's uncle in order to proceed, so Dianne accommodated the need.

In many families, some of the relatives, most often the grandfather and father, try to appear stoic and calm while facing the new and frightening experience of learning how to cope with the special needs their child will have. But clearly, this family was not concerned about the cleft. Dianne wondered if they did not perhaps understand that the infant would need surgery within a few days to close the cleft so he could swallow milk, and that he faced several more surgeries over the coming years. Parental fears about the child's pain and recovery are usually the main topic of discussion at the initial meeting. But, here was the family- smiling peacefully and joyfully.

After having a chance to explore offer her congratulations on the birth of the baby and talk for a few moments about the health of the baby with the young family, Dianne was able to learn an astonishing new cultural perspective on clefts of the lip and palate. The family explained to Dianne that the cleft on the baby was visible proof in this world that the baby had paid for the sins of an ancestor in the other world. He had sacrificed his health for the benefit of a family ancestor, so he was a family hero, at birth.

Dianne was concerned that the family might refuse surgery to repair the cleft, but they set her mind at ease immediately. Repairing the cleft would not be regarded by the family as reducing the sacrifice of the infant for his ancestor in any way, so medical intervention would be accepted without hesitation.

In working with people and their families, the culturally competent service provider is aware that beliefs he or she has found common among people in the past are not necessarily relevant to the person or family being helped today. There are vast differences between cultures (and individuals within cultures) on a number of levels[32].

These levels are:

1. Perceived seriousness of the problem: how much difficulty a client believes that a condition will cause versus how serious the condition appears to staff.

2. Perceived benefit of taking action: It may be a long time before a client is willing to seek help or to act on the advice the helping professional has offered. The reluctance to obtain help is related to the degree of difficulty that the conditions causes now (to the client) versus the degree of difficulty that treatment would cause (from the client's perspective).

---

[32] Spector, R. Cultural Diversity in Health and Illness

3. Modifying Factors: These may be either situational or belief based. Such factors include: that the client may not understand the poor outcome they will face down the road if they do not follow advice; they may be related to a fatalistic acceptance that "that is just the way things are"; or it just may be that the client knows that the advice-giver will not be there to deal with any adverse outcomes that may arise after the client takes the expert advice.

4. Cultural beliefs that differ from that of the provider: Sometimes the provider will have to accept that the beliefs of a person mean that they are willing to live under conditions quite different than those the helping provider wants to help the client obtain.

5. Socio-economic factors: There may be economic reasons for not taking action, or for failing to follow through on advice or instructions from helping professionals.

6. Communication: While helping professionals are widely known to ask personal questions of all kinds, clients may have low tolerance for what seems to them to be an unwelcome intrusion into their personal space.

Whatever the issues that arise between the client and the helpful service provider, the client has the right to keep his or her beliefs, and to act upon them. The culturally competent expert will have to seek and find ways to work with people that demonstrate a respect for the beliefs of the client in all situations.

What Dianne learned from the Hmong family's willingness to share their beliefs with her profoundly impacted her own ideas about disability. She was able to incorporate the attitude toward the clefting condition that the family shared with her, and to see the newborn in a new light, as a powerful force for good in the world. This carried over into her work with other families, and she shared the story with many young families over the years, to the betterment of everyone's perspective.

As we learned from the Hmong family, it is possible to fully accept and appreciate the benefit of a disability or condition, and still take action to accommodate the person so that they will find barriers to full participation in school, work and social settings removed.

Below we will show a number of categories, and then describe potential accommodations and resources for further investigation.

Everyone who is interested in barrier free living will want to add these pages – and others they may find online- to the large three-ring binder filled with accommodation resources that they already started.

Below you will find a set of resource links to help you get started on your binder. Let's look first at Assistive Technology to clarify its role in education and work.

ASSISTIVE TECHNOLOGY

Congress, recognizing the importance Assistive Technology (AT) can play in the lives of individuals with disabilities, first defined the terms assistive technology device and assistive technology service in the Technology-Related Assistance for Individuals with Disabilities Act of 1988 (P.L. 100-407). These definitions were later adopted in the Individuals with Disabilities Education Act, or IDEA, (P.L. 101-476) and the 1997 amendments (P.L. 105-17).

The IDEA defines an assistive technology device as "any item, piece of equipment or product system, whether acquired commercially of the shelf, modified, or customized, that is used to increase, maintain, or improve functional capabilities of a child with a disability." 20 USC § 1401(1). This definition is broad and includes a range of devices from low technology to high technology including computer hardware and software.

The definition of an assistive technology service as it appears in IDEA is "any service that directly assists an individual with a disability in the selection, acquisition, or use of an assistive technology device. Specifically these services include:

☐ The evaluation of the (technology) needs of the child, including a functional evaluation of the child 4in the child's customary environment:

☐ Purchasing, leasing or otherwise providing for the acquisition of assistive technology devices by children with disabilities.

☐ Selecting, designing, fitting, customizing, adapting, applying, maintaining, repairing, or replacing assistive technology devices;

☐ Coordinating and using other therapies, interventions, or services with assistive technology devices, such as those associated with existing education and rehabilitation plans and programs;

☐ Training or technical assistance for professionals (including individuals providing education or rehabilitation services), employers, or other individuals who provide services to, employ, or otherwise are substantially involved in the major life functions of a child with a disability. 20 USC § 1401(2)

☐ School districts are responsible for helping a child with a disability select and acquire an appropriate assistive technology device and assisting in training them to use the device.

The number of opportunities to include assistive technology devices and/or adaptive equipment in a child's educational environment is virtually limitless. Depending on the student's abilities and needs, there are a wide variety of items commercially available that could prove beneficial. Recognizing that each child is an individual with a unique learning style, there are an infinite number of modifications that could be made to existing equipment and equally endless possibilities for inventing and fabricating a custom assistive device.

The following categories of education-related technology are intended to provide a general guide of a variety of applications. Although these are not all inclusive, perhaps they will help the reader identify areas in which assistive technology could benefit the student.

☐ **Sensory enhancers** help students with sensory deficiencies to access their environments. Examples of this type of assistive technology would include augmentative communication devices, text magnifiers, scanners with speech synthesizers and voice analyzers

☐ **Keyboard adaptations and emulators** are alternatives to the standard computer keyboard used for inputting data. This category of

AT would include such items as joysticks, light pens, touch screens, touch sensitive keyboard pad, etc.

☐ **Environmental controls and manipulators** modify the operation of a device to compensate for environmental restrictions caused by a disability. Adaptations of light switches, timers, and telephones; robotics, additional external switches which can be activated by pressure, eyebrows or breath; Text Telephones (TTY's); and control mechanisms with sonar sensing devices are some of the many examples of AT that enable people with disabilities to control their environment.

☐ **Instructional uses of technology** such as specifically designed computer software, enable students with disabilities to receive full and equal educational opportunities. There is a wide variety of software available from practice drills to computer-assisted instructional programs.

☐ **Motivational devices** encourage the student to interact with his or her environment through exploration, manipulation and play. This category includes many types of toys and games which are commercially available "off the shelf", or which can be easily adapted.

Very often, battery operated toys are the easiest to modify so they will respond to a particular switch or chosen stimulus.

☐ **Mobility devices** include those devices that assist a student to help them get around in the school building and participate in student activities. Examples include such things as self-propelled walkers, manual or powered wheelchairs, and powered recreational vehicles like bikes or scooters. Mobility is also a standard term for specialized training and aids used by individuals who are visually impaired or blind.

☐ **Self Care** aids are necessary for some students who require assistance with activities like feeding, dressing, and toileting. Devices that help with self care include such things as robotics, electric feeders, adapted utensils, specially designed toilet seats, and aids for tooth-brushing, washing, dressing, and grooming.

Any of these devices can play an important role in classroom instruction and the student's education. These are but a few examples of the types of technology that can be provided by the local school district for the child.

There are three places in the IEP where assistive technology may be included.

1.   Assistive technology can be a part of the annual goals and short term objectives on an IEP . How assistive technology will contribute to achieving the goal and objectives must be clearly stated. The inclusion of assistive technology in the IEP requires an explanation of how and why the technology will be used to accomplish a particular goal. A goal, which includes AT, should indicate that the device will be part of conditions needed to acquire an academic or social skill. An annual goal for the IEP should express: 1) an estimate of what the student can accomplish in a skill area during the course of one year, 2) under what conditions the skill is to be developed, and 3) what criteria will be used to indicate whether or not the skill has been learned.

2.   The list of supplementary aids and services necessary to maintain the student in the least restrictive environment. Students with disabilities are guaranteed the right to placement in the educational setting which is the least restrictive environment. In order to be successful in the least restrictive environment, students

are to be afforded whatever supplementary aids and services necessary. Among the supplementary aids that may allow a student to remain in a less restrictive environment are a variety of assistive devices that compensate for disability and allow the student to perform educational and social tasks.

3.   The list of related services necessary for the student to benefit from his or her education is not exhaustive and includes many developmental, corrective, or support services. It is through this provision in the law that many school districts are providing students with disabilities assistive technology devices and services. Related services must be provided to a student with a disability at no cost to the parent or guardian.

For students to be successful with AT devices, they need to receive training on the use of the equipment. Training to use a computer, an augmentative communication device, or large print viewer, can occur as a related service that supports the student's educational program. Training on AT devices can be written into the IEP as a related service.

Assistive Technology Database [www.ableproject.org]

The mission of the Able Project is to provide a network where people with disabilities and their loved ones can effortlessly research, compare, locate and obtain mobility and assistive products, thereby helping them to lead more independent_lives.

AbleProject.org will utilize the power of the World Wide Web to:
- Help people learn about the available assistive equipment that include specialty designed computer keyboards, speech software, wheelchairs, scooters, commode chairs, bathing aids, modified vehicles.
- Let people do *comparison-shopping* to find the most affordable price and save money.

The Family Village www.familyvillage.wisc.edu

A global community that integrates information, resources, and communication opportunities on the Internet for persons with cognitive and other disabilities, for their families, and for those that provide them services and support.

Our community includes informational resources on specific diagnoses, communication connections, adaptive products and technology, adaptive recreational activities, education, worship, health issues, disability-related media and literature, and much, much more!

National Council on Independent Living http://www.ncil.org/
This is a membership organization that advances independent living and the rights of people with disabilities through consumer-driven advocacy. NCIL envisions a world in which people with disabilities are valued equally and participate fully.

Untangling The Web http://www.icdi.wvu.edu/others.htm
This is a comprehensive list of all lists! It provides pointers to many disability sites for General Information, Disability legislation, education, disability categories, information technology resources, assistive technology resources medical resources, agencies programs and services.

Matching Person and Technology
 http://members.aol.com/IMPT97/MPT.html
    This site offers information on training opportunities, book, CDs for purchase and other material that are of interest when a person is just starting to look for new technologies that might remove barriers in their life.

BARRIER FREE EDUCATION

Barrier Free Education (Link) http://barrier-free.arch.gatech.edu/
    Students with disabilities struggle with many barriers in their academic career. Teachers also struggle with ways to help these students

learn. Making some small accommodations in the classroom can help significantly.

This link provides some academic areas in which students face barriers coupled with ways for teachers to help their students using assistive technologies and other methods. Most of the accommodations are for science and math, but there some additional resources for computers and classroom learning as well as Distance Learning.

AIDS AND HIV www.jan.wvu.edu/media/HIV.html

JAN's Accommodation and Compliance Series is designed to help employers determine effective accommodations and comply with Title I of the Americans with Disabilities Act (ADA). Each publication in the series addresses a specific medical condition and provides information about the condition, ADA information, accommodation ideas, and resources for additional information.

AMPUTEE

Amputation means loss or absence of all or part of a limb. According to the National Limb Loss Information Center, there were 1,285,000 persons in the U.S. living with the limb loss (excluding fingers and toes) in 1996. The prevalence rate in 1996 was 4.9 per 1,000 persons. The incidence rate was 46.2 per 100,000 persons with dysvascular disease, 5.86 per 100,000 persons secondary to trauma, 0.35 per 100,000 secondary to malignancy of a bone or joint. The birth prevalence of

congenital limb deficiency in 1996 was 25.64 per 100,000 live births. The

prevalence rate is highest among people aged 65 years and older – about

19.4 per 1,000. Although congenital amputation rates have remained

consistent for several decades, dysvascular amputations have increased

significantly. Dysvascular refers to limb loss associated with vascular

conditions, mainly diabetes. Traumas resulting in limb loss or cancer

have been decreasing, however, war related injuries will change that

trend.

The following is a quick overview of some of the job accommodations

that might be useful for employees with amputation. To discuss an

accommodation situation with a consultant, contact JAN directly. In

general the following ideas may be of help.

Gross Motor Impairment:

- Modify the work-site to make it accessible
- Provide parking close to the work-site
- Provide an accessible entrance
- Install automatic door openers
- Provide an accessible restroom and break room

- Provide an accessible route of travel to other work areas used by the employee
- Modify the workstation to make it accessible
- Adjust desk height if wheelchair or scooter is used
- Make sure materials and equipment are within reach range
- Move workstation close to other work areas, break rooms and restrooms

Fine Motor Impairment:

- Implement ergonomic workstation design,
- Provide alternative computer and telephone access
- Provide sensitivity training to coworkers and supervisors

Upper Extremity Amputations (finger, hand, or arm):

- Keyboard/data entry—One-handed keyboards, typing tutorials for one-hand or missing digits, speech recognition software, large-key keyboards, foot mouse, touchpads, trackballs and head pointing systems
- Writing—Grip aids-writing cuffs, action arm orthotic devices, recoding devices for note taking, note-takers and clipboards
- Telephone use—Speaker-phones, telephones with programmable number storage, phone holders and telephone headsets
- Tool use—Grasping cuffs, grasping orthoses, ergonomically designed tools, vibration dampening tool wraps and gloves, vises, positioners, foot controls, pistol grip attachments and digital distance measuring devices
- Lifting items—Portable material lift equipment, tailgate lifts, hoists and lift-tables

- Carrying items—Lightweight carts,shoulder bags and powered carts or scooters with carrying baskets
- Filing papers—lateral files, carousel-rotary files, reduce the number of files per drawer, and rulers as pry-bars
- House-keeping/cleaning—Lightweight vacuum cleaners, back-pack vacs, long-handed cleaning aids and grasping cuffs
- Driving—Steering knobs, power assisted steering, grip gloves, steering wheel covers and remote controlled engine starters

Lower Extremity Amputations (toe, finger, or leg):

- Climbing—Stair-lifts, wheelchair platform lifts, climbing wheelchairs, rolling safety ladders with handrails, work platforms, and hydraulic personnel lifts.
- Standing—Sit/stand stools, stand supports, task stools, anti-fatigue matting, and rest breaks.
- Lifting/carrying—Material handling lifts, cranes, hoists, powered carts/scooters, hydraulic lift carts, lift-tables, lightweight carts with large wheels, and tailgate lifts.
- Driving—Hand controls, automatic clutching systems, left-foot gas pedals, automatic transmissions, and designated parking.
- Walking—Canes, crutches, rolling walkers with seats, wheelchairs, and powered wheelchairs/scooters.

Resources Specifically for People with Amputations:

Amputee Coalition of America

900 East Hill Avenue, Suite 285

Knoxville, TN 37915-2568

Toll Free: (888) AMP-KNOW (888 267-5669)

Direct: (865) 524-8772

TTY: (865) 525-4512

Fax: (865) 525-7917

http://amputee-coalition.org

Amputee Online.Com

http://amputee-online.com

Limbs for Life Foundation

5929 N. May, Suite 511

Oklahoma City, OK 73112

Toll Free: (888) 235-5462

Direct: (405) 843-5174

Fax: (405) 843-5123

Email: admin@limbsforlife.org

http://www.limbsforlife.org

National Amputation Foundation

40 Church Street

Malverne, NY 11565

Phone: (516) 887-3600

Fax: (516) 887-3667

E-mail: amps76@aol.com

http://www.nationalamputation.org/

National Limb Loss Information Center

900 East Hill Ave. Suite 285

Knoxville, TN 37909

888-267-5669

http://www.amputee-coalition.org

O&P Digital Technologies

6830 NW 11th Place, Suite A

Gainesville, FL 32605

Toll Free: (800) 876-7740

Direct: (352) 331-3741

Fax: (352) 332-8074

E-Mail: info@oandp.com

http://oandp.com

Amputee Coalition of America http://www.amputee-coalition.org/aca_mission.html

Mission: To reach out to people with limb loss and to empower them through education, support and advocacy. This includes access to, and delivery of, information, quality care, appropriate devices, reimbursement, and the services required to lead empowered lives.

BLIND OR LOW VISION

People who are blind or who have low vision have a number of low cost accommodations that can remove barriers from educational and work settings. These include the following.

For people with Low Vision: use of a lighted magnifier and large print paper. Pre-printed material can be enlarged on a photocopier. The computer can be set to enhance size and 'black background" to improve visibility of the written word. Taking frequent rests to give the eyes a chance to recover iseffective, as are utilizing auditory readers on the computer.

People who are blind may use auditory readers as well, Braille formatted documents or computerized readers capable of reading websites and documents to the computer user.

Resources include:

The American Foundation for the Blind http://www.afb.org/default.asp
Expanding a wide range of possibilities for people with vision loss.

American Council for the Blind http://www.acb.org/

This service provides general information about the Council, including recent issues of our monthly publication, The Braille Forum.

Book Share   www.bookshare.org

Subscription service for books in digital accessible format.

BRAIN INJURY

According to Traumatic Brain Injury Recovery Center (2006), "TBI is any injury to the brain caused by trauma to the head. If there is trauma to the brain, but the skull is not broken, the TBI is known as a closed head injury. This could occur, for example, if a person in an automobile accident hits his head on the steering wheel, but does not have a skull fracture. If an object such as a bullet penetrates the skull and injures the brain, the TBI is known as a penetrating head injury."

There are several different types of TBI (TBI Recovery Center, 2006):

Concussion: A concussion is the most minor and common type of TBI. A concussion is caused when the brain receives a somewhat minor trauma from an impact, such as a hit to the head by an object or person or from a sudden change in momentum, such as a fall. It may or may not result in a short loss of consciousness (not exceeding 20 minutes) and can be diagnosed by observing common symptoms such as headache, confusion, and vomiting. Difficulty with thinking skills (e.g., difficulty "thinking straight," memory problems, poor judgment, poor attention

273

span, a slowed thought processing speed) (Brain Injury Association of America, 2006a; TBI Recovery Center, 2006).

Skull Fracture: A skull fracture occurs when the skull cracks or breaks. A depressed skull fracture occurs when pieces of broken skull press into the tissue of the brain. A penetrating skull fracture occurs when something pierces the skull and injures the brain (Brain Injury Association of America, 2006a; TBI Recovery Center, 2006).

Contusion: A contusion is bruising or bleeding of the brain (Brain Injury Association of America, 2006a; TBI Recovery Center, 2006). Hematoma: A hematoma is a collection of blood inside the body (Brain Injury Association of America, 2006a; TBI Recovery Center, 2006). The following sites are recommended for additional information.

Be Independent. http://www.bindependent.com/
This web site takes an up-close look at specific brain injury problems, providing crisp, clear definitions and coping strategies. Currently under the microscope: improving memory and managing medications.

Frequently Asked Questions About Traumatic Brain Injury
    http://www.tbihelp.org/

CANCER www.jan.wvu.edu/media/Cancer.html
The ADA does not contain a list of medical conditions that constitute disabilities. Instead, the ADA has a general definition of disability that

each person must meet (EEOC, 1992). Therefore, some people with cancer will have a disability under the ADA and some will not. Here are suggestions for accommodations for people living with cancer.

CEREBRAL PALSY

Cerebral palsy is a term used to describe a group of chronic conditions affecting body movement and muscle coordination. It is caused by damage to one or more specific areas of the brain, usually occurring during fetal development; before, during, or shortly after birth; or during infancy. Thus, these disorders are not caused by problems in the muscles or nerves. Instead, faulty development or damage to motor areas in the brain disrupt the brain's ability to adequately control movement and posture (United Cerebral Palsy, 2001).

"Cerebral" refers to the brain and "palsy" to muscle weakness/poor control. CP itself is not progressive; however, secondary conditions, such as muscle spasticity, can develop, which may get better over time, get worse, or remain the same. CP is not communicable; it is not a disease (United Cerebral Palsy, 2001).

A good list of accommodations for work situations is provided as well as background information. www.jan.wvu.edu/media/CP.html

These include the following Accommodation Ideas:

Activities of Daily Living:

• Providing close proximity to restrooms

• Adapting accessibility features in the restrooms

• Allowing use of personal care attendants

• Allowing use of a service animal

• Allowing extra time for activities of daily living (ADL)

Fine Motor Impairment:

• Modifying workstation design

• Using alternative computer input devices/software

• Using telephone assistance devices

• Using writing aids and grips

• Adjusting filing/storage systems

Gross Motor Impairment:

• Maintaining unobstructed hallways, aisles and other building egress

• Assigning workspace in close proximity to office machines

• Modifying workstation design and height

• Providing lightweight doors or automatic door openers

• Removing building barriers to access including close designated parking, accessible router and entrances

Cognitive Impairment:

• Using computer software programs for self-editing, word prediction, grammar/spell checkers, etc.

• Providing electronic organizers, posting of notes/reminders

• Allowing extra time to complete work assignments

Communication Activities:

• Developing a plan and providing equipment for safe evacuation

• Alerting the fire department of probable location of the individual with mobility impairments in case of emergency

• Providing speech augmentation devices

COGNITIVE DISABILITY OR DEVELOPMENTAL DISABILITY

The Job Accommodation Network (www.jan.wvu.edu) provides an extensive series of handouts to assist with job accommodations across disability types. Here are their recommendations for cognitive impairment.

Maintaining Concentration:

• Reduce distractions in the work area

• Provide space enclosures or a private office

• Allow for use of white noise or environmental sound machines

• Allow the employee to play soothing music using a cassette player and headset

• Increase natural lighting or provide full spectrum lighting

• Reduce clutter in the employee's work environment

• Plan for uninterrupted work time

• Divide large assignments into smaller tasks and steps

• Restructure job to include only essential functions

Staying Organized and Meeting Deadlines:

- Make daily TO-DO lists and check items off as they are completed
- Use several calendars to mark meetings and deadlines
- Remind employee of important deadlines via memos or e-mail or weekly supervision
- Use a watch or pager with timer capability and electronic organizers
- Divide large assignments into smaller tasks and steps
- Assign a mentor to assist employee determining goals and provide daily guidance
- Schedule weekly meetings with supervisor, manager or mentor to determine if goals are being met

Handling Memory Deficits:

- Allow the employee to tape record meetings
- Provide type written minutes of each meeting
- Use notebooks, calendars, or sticky notes to record information for easy retrieval
- Provide written as well as verbal instructions
- Allow additional training time
- Provide written checklists
- Provide environmental cues to assist in memory for locations of items, such as labels, color coding, or bulletin boards
- Post instructions over all frequently used equipment

Handling Problem Solving Deficits:

- Provide picture diagrams of problem solving techniques, i.e. flow charts
- Restructure the job to include only essential functions
- Assign a supervisor, manager or mentor to be available when the employee has questions

Working Effectively with Supervisors:
- Provide positive praise and reinforcement
- Provide written job instructions
- Write clear expectations of responsibilities and the consequences of not meeting them
- Allow for open communication to managers and supervisors
- Establish written long term and short term goals
- Develop strategies to deal with problems before they arise
- Provide written work agreements
- Develop a procedure to evaluate the effectiveness of the accommodation

Handling Stress and Emotions:
- Provide praise and positive reinforcement
- Refer to counseling and employee assistance programs
- Allow telephone calls during work hours to doctors and others for needed support
- Provide sensitivity training to coworkers

- Allow the employee to take a break to use stress management techniques to deal with frustration

Handling Change:

- Recognize that a change in the office environment or of supervisors may be difficult
- Maintain open channels of communication between the employee and the new and old supervisor in order to ensure an effective transition
- Provide weekly or monthly meetings with the employee to discuss workplace issues and productions levels

Maintaining Stamina During the Workday:

- Flexible scheduling
- Allow longer or more frequent work breaks
- Provide additional time to learn new responsibilities
- Provide self-paced workload
- Provide backup coverage for when the employee needs to take breaks
- Allow for time off for counseling
- Allow for use of supportive employment and job coaches
- Allow employee to work from home during part of the day
- Provide for job sharing opportunities
- Part-time work schedules

Other specialty websites include the following:

Special_Educator's_Web_Pages

http://www.geocities.com/Athens/Styx/7315/

This site is written by a Special Education teacher. It includes information and links for lesson plans, behavior management, teaching, inclusion, law, links to free things, research and scholarship, grants, parent and student support, organizations, IEPs, learning and the like.

COMPUTER_ACCOMMODATIONS

http://www.icdi.wvu.edu/others.htm#g8

- AbleLink. www.qwerty.com Computer and PDA access.
- Ainsworth & Partners, Inc.. Keyboard training software for people with special needs.
- EyeTech Digital Systems. EyeTechDS.com offers a hands free computing product for disabled people called Quick Glance. The Quick Glance system makes it possible to operate a computer with eye movement only.
- Gus Communications Multimedia Speech System. Source for speech output and computer access software www.gusinc.com
- IBM Special Needs Solutions. Information on IBM's accessibility products and activities.
- ifbyphone.com Internet service by voice from any phone. Send and receive Emails, browse and search, schedule wake-up and Email alert calls as well as voice chat rooms and games.

- o IntegrityConsulting.US Assistive technology for people with a wide range of disabilities--minimal to severe.
- o Laureate Learning Systems. Software for people with special needs. www.lisys.com
- o Microsoft Accessability. Accessibility features in Microsoft products.www. microsoft.com/enable
- o Minomech Enterprises. Providing access to computers and other high-technology for individuals with special needs. Minomech.com
- o Synapse Adaptive. Adaptive technology, primarily software. Emphasis on speech recognition, learning, and ADA. www.synapseadaptive.com
- o Unbounded Access. Technology and services to make Internet sites and company intranets accessible to people with disabilities. www.ubaccess.com
- o Webbie. A web browser for blind and visually-impaired people, especially those using screen readers. www.webbie.org.uk

DEAF OR HARD OF HEARING

Hearing Exchange www.hearingexchange.com

A community for people with hearing loss, parents of deaf and hard of hearing children and professionals who work with them.

SHHH: Self Help for Hard of Hearing People, Inc. www.shhh.org

A nonprofit, educational organization, is dedicated to the well-being of people of all ages and communication styles who do not hear well.

TTY Frequently Asked Questions   http://www.zak.co.il/deaf-info/old/tty_faq.html

Information on TTYs and how to adjust them so that they work better.

United TTY Sales and Service   www.unitedtty.com

Assistive technology for persons with hearing impairments.

EMPLOYMENT ASSISTANCE

Job Accommodation Network http://www.jan.wvu.edu/portals/faqs.html

The Job Accommodation Network is a **free** service of the Office of Disability Employment Policy (ODEP) of the U.S. Department of Labor. JAN is one of several ODEP technical assistance projects. JAN represents the most comprehensive resource for job accommodations available.

JAN's mission is to facilitate the employment and retention of workers with disabilities by providing employers, employment providers, people with disabilities, their family members and other interested parties with information on job accommodations, self-employment and small business opportunities.

eSight Careers Network   www.esightcareers.net

Career development and management resources, networking, job listings for people who are blind or have low vision.

The Low Vision Gateway http://www.lowvision.org/

Internet resources and information for people with low vision.

EPILEPSY www.jan.wvu.edu/media/epilepsy.html

Information about Epilepsy and work accommodations are provided through this Department of Labor funded page.

SERVICE DOGS

Canine Companions http://www.caninecompanions.org/

Canine Companions for Independence® is a national nonprofit organization that enhances the lives of children and adults with
 disabilities by providing highly-trained assistance dogs and ongoing
 support to ensure quality partnerships.

HEPATITIS www.jan.wvu.edu/media/hep.html

Learn the A-B-C's of Hepatitis.

LEARNING DISABILITY AND ATTENTION DEFICIT

AHEAD- The association on Higher Education and Disability
 http://www.ahead.org/

AHEAD is the premiere professional association committed to full participation of persons with disabilities in postsecondary education. AHEAD

- values diversity, personal growth and development, and creativity

- promotes leadership and exemplary practices
- provides professional development and disseminates information
- orchestrates resources through partnership and collaboration

AHEAD dynamically addresses current and emerging issues with respect to disability, education, and accessibility to achieve universal access. Since 1977 AHEAD has delivered quality training to higher education personnel through conferences, workshops, publications and consultation.

PERVASIVE DEVELOPMENTAL DISABILITY

Autism   http://www.autismtoday.com/aboutus.htm

With over 2,500 pages of content which is growing daily, Autism Today is the largest autism resource online and one of the leading autism and Aspergers resource distributor in the world.

SLEEP DISORDER

http://www.sleepdisordersguide.com/

About problems with sleeping and how to manage them.

WHEELCHAIR ACCOMMODATIONS/ RESOURCES

National Spinal Cord Injury Association http://www.spinalcord.org/

This group educates and empowers survivors of spinal cord injury and disease to achieve and maintain the highest levels of independence, health and personal fulfillment. We fulfill this mission by providing an innovative Peer Support Network and by raising awareness about spinal cord injury and disease through education. Our education programs are developed to address information and issues important to our constituency, policy makers, the general public, and the media, and including injury prevention, improvements in medical, rehabilitative and supportive services, research and public policy formulation.

360-Degrees http://www.360-mag.com/home.cfm
360◦ USA Inc is your Online Source for the Disability Community, 360◦ USA Inc. is an interactive "ezine" that challenges the traditional views of people with disabilities. Our mix of insightful articles, convenient shopping and unique sections positions us as a favorite online source for information and entertainment.

Use the websites mentioned above only as a starting place as you search for resources to help you with your efforts to remove barriers to community life.

References and Recommended Reading

Bacharach, P. & Baratz, M.. (1970). Power and poverty. New York: Oxford University Press.

Bandura, A. (1997). Self-Efficacy. Insights, The Harvard Mental Health Letter, Vol 13, No.9. Harvard Medical School.

Bannerman, D., Sheldon, J., Sherman, J., & Harchik, A. (1990). Balancing the right to habilitation with the right to personal liberties: The rights of people with developmental disabilities to eat too many doughnuts and take a nap. Journal of Applied Behavior Analysis, 23 (1), 78-89.

Bellah, R., Madsen, R., Sullivan, W., Swidler, A., & Tipton, S. (1991). The good society. New York: Knopf.

Berger, PI, & Neuhouse, R.J. (1977) To Empower People: The Role of Mediating Structures in Public Policy. Washington, D.C.: American Enterprise Institute.

Braddock, D. (1998). The state of the states in developmental disabilities. Washington, D.C.: American Association on Mental Retardation.

Bradley, V., & Knoll, J. (1990). Shifting paradigms in services to people with developmental disabilities. Baltimore: Paul H. Brooks.

Bradley, V., Ashbaugh, J., & Blaney, B. (1992). Creating supports for people with developmental disabilities: A mandate for change at many levels. Baltimore: Paul H. Brooks.

Callahan, M. (2000). Personal budgets: The future of funding? Indianapolis: United Cerebral Palsy Association.

Callahan, M., & Mank, D. (1998). Choice and control of employment forpeople with disabilities. In T. Nerney & D. Shumway (Eds.) The importance of income. (pp. 16-33).
Concord, NH: Robert Wood Johnson Foundation.

Campbell, D.T., & Fiske, D.W. (1959). Convergent and discriminant validation by the multi-trait-multi-method matrix. Psychological Bulletin, 56, 81-105.

Campbell, J., & Oliver, M. (1996). Disability politics. Understanding our past, changing our future. London: Routledge.

Cone, A. (1994). Reflections on self-advocacy: Voices for choices. Mental Retardation, 32, 444 -446.

Cone, A. (1997). The beat goes on. Lessons learned from rhythms of the self-advocacy movement. Mental Retardation. 35, 144-146.

Cone, A. (1999). Profile of advisors to self-advocacy groups for people with mental retardation. Mental Retardation, 37, 308-318.

Cook, T.D., & Campbell, D.T. (1979). Quasi-experimentation: Design and analysis issues for field settings. Chicago: Rand McNally

Corrigan, P., Faber, D., Rashid, F. & Leary, M. (1999). The construct validity of empowerment among consumers of mental health services. Schizophrenia Research, 38, 77-84.

Dahl, R. (1961). Who governs? Democracy and power in an American city. New Haven: Yale University Press.

Danforth, S. (1995). Toward a critical theory approach to lives considered emotionally disturbed. Behavioral Disorders, 20 (2), 136-143.

DeVaris, J. (1994). The dynamics of power in psychotherapy. Psychotherapy, 31, 588-593.

Diller, M. (1998). Dissonant disability policies: The tensions between the ADA and federal disability benefit programs. Texas Law Review, 76, 1003- 1082.

Dokecki, P., (1996). The tragi-comic professional: Basic considerations for ethical reflective-generative practice. Pittsburg, PA: Duquesne University Press.

Dryden, W., & Feltham, C. (Eds.) (1992). Psychotherapy and its discontents. Philadelphia: Open University Press.

Dziuban, C.D. & Shirley, E.C, (1974). When is a correlation matrix appropriate for factor analysis? Psychological Bulletin, 81, 358-361.

Edgerton, R.B. (1990). Quality of life from a longitudinal perspective. In R.L. Schalock (Ed.), Quality of life: Perspectives and issues (pp. 149-160). Washington, D.C.: American Association on Mental Retardation.

Friere, P. (1972). Cultural action for freedom. Harmondsworth, Middex: Penguin books.

Gaventa, J. (1980). Power and powerlessness: Quiescence and rebellion in an Appalachian valley. Chicago: University of Chicago Press.

Geller, J., Brown, J-M., Fisher, W., Grudzinskas, A., & Manning, T.(1998). A national survey of "consumer empowerment" at the state level. Psychiatric Services, 49 (4) 87-92.

Hagner, D., & Marrone, J. (1995). Empowerment issues in services individuals with disabilities. Journal of Disability Policy Studies, 6 (2), 17-35.

Hardy, C., & Leiba-O'Sullivan, S. (1998). The power behind empowerment: Implications for research and practice. Human Relations, 51 (4), 451 – 583.

Haugaard, M. (1997) The Constitution Of Power. Manchester University Press: Manchester.

Heifetz, R. (1994). Values in leadership: Leadership without easy answers. Cambridge: The Belknap Press of Harvard University Press.

Heller, K. (1989). The return to community. American Journal of Community Psychology, 17 (1), 102-112.

Hess, R. (1984). Thoughts on empowerment. In Hess (Ed.), Studies in empowerment (pp. 227 – 230). Boston: Haworth Press.

Holburn, S. (2000). New paradigm for some, old paradigm for others. Mental Retardation, 31, 530.

Holmes, J., & Lindley, R. (1989). The values of psychotherapy. New York: Oxford University Press.

Kachigan, S. (1986). Statistical analysis: An interdisciplinary introduction to univariate and mulitvariate methods. New York : Radius Press.

Le Bosse, Y., Lavallee, M., Lacerte, D., Dube, N., Nadeau, J., Porcher, E., & Vandette, L. (1998). Is community participation empirical evidence for psychological empowerment? A distinction between passive and active participation. Social Work & Social Sciences Review, 8 (1), 59-82.

Lewin, M. (1979). Understanding psychological research. New York: John Wiley & Sons.

Longhurst, N. (1994). The self-advocacy movement by people with developmental disabilities. Washington, D.C.: American Association on Mental Retardation

Lukes, S. (1974). Power: A radical view. In Anthony Giddens, (Ed.), Studies in sociology (pp. 9 - 64). London: Macmillan Press, LTD.

McMillan, J.H. (1996) Educational Research (2nd ed.). New York: Harper Collins College.

Mack, J. (1994). Power, powerlessness, and empowerment in psychotherapy. Psychiatry, 57, 178-198.

Mackelprang, R., & Salsgiver, R. (1999). Disability: A diversity model approach in human service practice. Pacific Grove, CA: Brooks-Cole Publishing Co.

Mair, K. (1992). The myth of therapist expertise. In W. Drydan & C. Feltham (Eds.), Psychotherapy and its discontents (pp. 135-159). Philadelphia: Open University Press.

Marrone, J. (1994). If everybody is already doing it, how come it never gets done? Psychosocial Rehabilitation Journal, 18 (2), 73-76.

Missouri Division of Mental Retardation/Developmental Disability Website. (1998). [On-line] Available.http://www.moddmh.state.mo.us/. Accessed January, 2001.

Moore, D.S. (1985). Statistics, concepts, and controversies. New York:Freeman.

Murphy, S. (1998). Counselor and client views of vocational rehabilitation success and failure: A qualitative study. Rehabilitation Counseling Bulletin, 3, 185-197.

Nagler, M. (1990). Perspectives on disability. Palo Alto: Health Markets Research. National Council on Disability. (1999). Progress Report. [On-line]. Available: http://www.ncd.gov/mandate.htm. Accessed June, 1999.

Neath, J. (1997). Social causes of impairment, disability, and abuse. Journal of Disability Policy Studies, 8 (1-2), 195-230.

Neath, J., & Schriner, K. (1998). Power to people with disabilities. Empowerment issues in employment programming. Disability and Society, 13 (2), 217-228.

Nelis, T. (1994). Self-advocacy: Realizing a dream. Impact, 7 (1), 1.

Nerney, T. (1998). The Poverty of human services: An introduction in T. Nerney & D. Shumway (Eds.), The Importance of Income (pp. 2 – 14). Concord, NH: Self-Determination for Persons with Developmental Disabilities.

Newbrough, J. (1995). Toward community: A third position. American Journal of Community Psychology, 23 (1), 9-30.

Newbrough, J., Dokecki, P., & O'Gorman, R. (1993). Communiogenesis: A conversation between theology and community psychology. Paper presented at the Society for Community Action and Research. Biennial Gathering Chicago.

O'Brien, J., & O'Brien, C. (1999). A little book about person centered planning. Toronto: Inclusion Press.

O'Brien, J. & O'Brien, C. (2000). The politics of person centered planning. Minneapolis: University of Minnesota.

Parenti, M. (1978). On power. New York: St.Martins Press.

Pederson, E., Chaikin, M., Koehler, D., Campbell, A., & Arcand, M. (1993). Strategies that close the gap between research, planning, and self-advocacy. In E. Sutton (Ed.), Older adults with developmental disabilities: Optimizing choice and change (235-242). Baltimore: Paul H. Brooks.

Peterson, N. A., & Zimmerman, M. A. (in press). Beyond the Individual:Toward a Nomological Network of Organizational Empowerment. American Journal of Community Psychology.

Pence, G. (1995). Classic cases in medical ethics (2nd ed.). New York: McGraw Hill.

Pierce, G.F. (1984). Activism that makes sense. Chicago: ACTAPublications.

Prilleltensky, I. (1997). Values, assumptions, and practices. American Psychologist, (7), 518-535.

Prouty, R., & Larkin, K. (Eds.), (1999). Report #52. Residential services for persons with developmental disabilities: Status and trends through 1998. Minneapolis: Research and Training Center on

Community Living. Institute on Community Integration. College of Education and Human Development. University of Minnesota.

The Developmental Disabilities Assistance and Bill of Rights Amendment. Public Law 100-146 (1987).

Robertson, A., & Minkler, B. (1994) New health promotion movement: A critical examination. Health Education Quarterly, 21, 295-312.

Rhodes, R. (1993). Mental retardation and sexual expression: An historical perspective. In R. Mackelprang & D. Valentine (Eds.). Sexuality and disability: A guide for human services practitioners (pp. 1 – 127). Binghamton, NY: Haworth Press

Richardson, F. (1995). Beyond relativism? Psychology and the moral dimension (Review of the book *Social Discourse and Moral Judgment*). Theory and Psychology, 5, 316 – 318.

Riger, S. (1993). What's wrong with empowerment? American Journal of Community Psychology, 21, 279-292.

Ryan, W. (1976). Blaming The Victim. Vintage Books: New York.

Sarason, S. (1981). Caring and compassion in clinical practice. San Francisco: Jossey-Bass.

Sarason, S. (1992). Series editor's preface. In: Crossing the river, by D. Schwartz. Pittsburg: Brookline Books.

Saucier, J., Kurtz, A., & Gilmer, D. (1996). Self-advocacy for self-advocates: A leadership guide. Brunswick: Center for Community Inclusion, University of Maine.

Schwartz, D. (1992). Crossing the river. Pittsburg: Brookline Books.

Seidman, E. (1983). Unexamined premises of social problem solving. In Seidman (Ed.), Handbook of social intervention (pp. 87- 125). Beverly Hills: Sage.

Senge, P. (1990) The fifth discipline: The art and practice of the learning organization. New York: Doubleday.

Serrano-Garcia, (1994). The ethics of the powerful and the power ethics. Presidential address of the Society for Research and Action at the annual meeting of the American Psychological Society, Toronto, Canada.

Spector, R. (1996) Cultural Divesity in Health and Illness, 4th ed. Appleton & Lange: Stamford, CT

Speer, P.W., & Hughey, J. (1995) Community Organizing: An Ecological Route to Empowerment and Power. American Journal of Community Psychology, Vol. 23, No. 5.

Speer, P. W. & Peterson, N. A. (2000). Psychometric properties of an empowerment scale: Testing cognitive, emotional, and behavioral domains. *Social Work Research*, 24, 109-118.

Spinelli, E. (1994). Demystifying theory. London: Constable.

State of Missouri People First Steering Committee. (2000). Minutes of the June, 2000 meeting. [On-line]. Available.
http:www.missouripeoplefirst.org, accessed July, 2000.

Sutherland, S. (1992). What goes wrong in the care and treatment of the mentally ill. In W. Dryden & C. Feltham (Eds.), Psychotherapy and its Discontents (pp.169-186). Bristol, PA: Open University Press.

Taylor, G. (1996a). Ethical issues in practice: Participatory social research and groups. Groupwork, 110-127

Taylor, G. (1996b). Empowerment, identity and participatory research: Using social action research to challenge isolation for deaf and hard of hearing people from minority communities. Disability and Society, 14 (3), 369-384.

Tyne, A. (1994). Taking responsibility and giving power. Disability and Society, 9, 249-252.

Wallerstein, N. (1992). Powerlessness, empowerment, and health: Implications for health promotion programs. American Journal of Health Promotion, 6. 197-204.

Ward, N., & Keith, K. (1996). Self-Advocacy: Foundation for quality of life. In R.L. Schalock (Ed.) Quality of life, Volume I. Conceptualization and measurement (pp. 5-10). Washington D.C: American Association on Mental Retardation.

West, M., & Parenti, W. (1992). Consumer choice and empowerment in supported employment services: Issues and strategies. Journal of the Association of Persons with Severe Handicaps, 17, 47-52.

Whitehead, T. (1999). Autonomy and Competency- self-determination in the lives of adults with developmental disabilities. Bioethics Forum, 15 (2), 19-30.

Whitehead, T. (2001). Analysis of Social Power In The Relationship Between People With Developmental Disabilities And Their Service System. A Dissertation.

Whitehead, T. & Hughey,J. (2004) Exploring Self Advocacy from a Social Power Perspective. Nova Science Publishers: New York

Williams, P., & Shoultz, B. (1982). We can speak for ourselves. Bloomington: Indiana University Press.

Wolfensberger, W. (1972). The principle of normalization in human services. Toronto: National Institute on Mental Retardation.

Zimmerman, M. (2000). Empowerment theory: Psychological, organizational, and community levels of analysis. In Rappaport, J. (Ed); Seidman, E.(Ed), Handbook of community psychology. (pp.43-63), Dordrecht, Netherlans: Kluwer Academic Publishers.

Note from the author:

Thank you for reading this book. I hope it was helpful to you on your journey, and I hope you will one day write a book that is more comprehensive and useful than this one was.

As Gandhi said, "Be the change you want to see in the world."

Go out and make a difference!

CPSIA information can be obtained at www.ICGtesting.com
Printed in the USA
242163LV00003B/47/P